AF505834

COORDINATING COMMITTEE
AN AUSTRIAN DELEGATION LOOKS AT WAR, TAXES AND REFORM, 1697–1703

BY

WILLIAM B. SLOTTMAN

EAST EUROPEAN MONOGRAPHS, BOULDER

DISTRIBUTED BY COLUMBIA UNIVERSITY PRESS, NEW YORK

1999

EAST EUROPEAN MONOGRAPHS, NO. DXXIV

Contents

Preface
The Genesis of the Manuscript

The present monograph is a valuable contribution to the history of the internal political structure of the Habsburg lands in Central Europe. The author studied a considerable number of relevant sources and assiduosly researched the rather complex topic. For unknown reasons the study remained unpublished. In my subsequent remarks I shall refer to it simply as the Deputatio. This was the project's working title in my correspondence with the author. On the basis of that exchange of thoughs I shall explain the genesis of the manuscript.

William B. Slottman was a distinguished historian who wrote important manuscripts about the late seventeenth century. Regrettably he did not live to see their publication. After his death on May 4, 1995, the manuscript of the present book was found among his papers. As I hope to show in my Preface, he had not planned to publish it, and after a considerable delay it now appears in print.

What is the Deputatio? Towards the end of the long war between Austria and the Ottoman Empire which started with the siege of Vienna in 1683, the emperor's financial difficulties had reached a critical stage. In order to organize the raising of much needed financial support, a separate institution, the Deputatio, was founded to coordinate the procedures. Each Habsburg territory in Central Europe was represented in the council which tried to distribute the burdens of the war as fairly as possible among the individual parts of the Habsburg monarchy according to their financial abilities. Ultimately the council dealt also with a multitude of other problems. Consequently its minutes are an outstanding source to assess the political structure of the Habsburg domains in Central Europe.

Bill Slottman recognized the importance of these minutes and, in conjunction with many other sources, used them to write the present monograph. Originally he intended to utilize the material only for his doctoral dissertation about the cultural context of the negotiations leading to the Peace of Carlowitz (1699) which ended the long war. While working on his dissertation, however, he decided to distill from the collected materials two particularly interesting topics and to deal with them in two substantial monographs. One study Bill Slottman devoted to the role of William 6th Baron Paget (1637-1713), English ambassador at Vienna, and later at Constantinople, as mediator in the negotiations leading to the Peace at Carlowitz; the other to the analysis of the significant work of the Deputatio which provided a better opportunity than any other institution to observe the trend to absolutism in the Habsburg monarchy.

In October, 1957, Bill Slottman decided to work on both topics simultaneously. He consistently adhered to this strategy until he completed his tasks in the fall of 1968. Occasionally he paid more attention to one topic tan the other, and ultimately the study of the Deputatio turned out to be much slimmer than the voluminous manuscript on Lord Paget which was not found among Bill Slottman's papers after his death.

As mentioned above, originally the minutes of the Deputatio were intended to serve only as one of the sources for the work on the negotiations leading to the Peace at Carlowitz. Bill Slottman, however, could not make all the excerpts from the European archives himself. Increasingly he was under pressure to be ready for the start of an academic career at the most advantageous moment. He only found time to look at the catalogues of archives, estimated the importance of their holdings, and then found research assistants who copied the documents he needed.

The work on the Deputatio produced unexpected problems. The minutes were particularly difficult to read, and hardly anyone was willing to copy their most important parts. Finally, however, a copy was made, partly at the end of 1957, and at last completed at the end of 1958. As additional material above all Bill Slottman needed the ambassadors' report of the Emperor's most important allies in the war. In his letters he wrote about the problem:

> "I am very much interested in the possibility of someone working in the Archive. If I receive the grant I mentioned I am thinking of having a whole run of the Dispacci microfilmed, and I shall need help putting the finishing touches to the Deputatio." (October 27, 1963)

In the meantime he had started writing the manuscript:

> "I shall have to make certain changes in direction and will have to spend more time brushing up the second briefer thing which I have to do -- the monograph on the Deputatio. I wouldn't be surprised at all to learn that there are a whole group of people working on that, but I will hope that the rumor factories are more efficient in Vienna than they are in the Anglo-Saxon world." (April 4, 1964)

As far as I know, at that time no one worked on the topic, but temporary difficulties occurred with the other book dealing with Lord Paget, the diplomat. In Berkeley, Bill Slottman had found someone to talk with who had extensive experience on an analogous topic:

> "The thing to do in this case will be to combine what I have already done, ... with thoughts that have been insprired by reading and talking with Hans Rosenberg." (June 20, 1964)

It is important to keep in mind that Bill Slottman was writing two manuscripts at the same time which together were somewhat over one thousand pages long. Naturally that delayed the completion of both manuscripts. In particular Bill Slottman was anxious to find out who had kept the minutes of the Deputatio, the central source of his monograph. During the copying process of the documents efforts had already been made to determine the authorship. Later on, one of the most experienced archivist of the Haus-, Hof-, and Staatsarchiv in Vienna worked for some time to discover the author's name. All efforts, however, remained unsuccessful. Bill Slottman was forced to write the manuscript without being able to identify the author of his most important source.

"I finally finished the Deputation and sent it off to Harvard. Since I have not heard for some time I can only hope that the answer will be favorable, though I am more than usually conscious of its shortcomings." (October 20, 1968)

"Harvard University Press reported ... that it was ready to publish my monograph on the Deputatio. I shall try to fis it up just a bit, but I am confident that by the beginning of the summer they will have settled down to printing it." (March 19, 1969)

Much to my regret I cannot recall the reason why the manuscript which he had submitted to Harvard University Press was not published. Despite its significance the manuscript never appeared in print during its author's life time. It is sad that he did not live to see the book. He deserved to be honored publicly for his great endeavor, the merit of his work, and its magnificent presentation.

In subsequent years Bill Slottman spoke rarely about problems of archival work and was, perhaps, embittered that his splendid efforts remained hidden from most of his colleagues. He began to doubt the meaning of the detailed, systematic archival work which he had done with so much elan and success as a young man.

Walter Leitsch

Introduction
Deputatio / Coordinating Committee

Our contemporaries have come to regard the committee as an institution and as an 'art form' with a good deal of suspicion. The mere mention of possible service on a committee is sufficient to arouse a wide variety of negative reactions and the expression of reluctance to serve. For committee work conjures up a most depressing prospect: the endless meetings, the interaction of verbose and trying personalities, the long and meandering discussion that inevitably produces little in the way of positive results. To some spirits more sensitive than the rest of the committee has come to be regarded as one of the most punishing penitential practices of our age, a discipline that yields little or nothing to the rigors of the Thebaid.

At the same time even those most antipathetic to committees usually have to admit that they are indispensable for the functioning of society. Without these small groups gathering with a bewildering variety of functions and aims -- discussion, study, investigation, planning, decision-making, and so on -- we would be unable to exist at the present level of social complexity. In such a perspective committee work ceases to be simply one of the most wearisome obligations imposed on human beings and becomes a positive contribution to mankinds' further development. But this recognition of the importance of committees, wrung from individuals much against their will, can hardly be taken to constitute a massive vote of confidence in the committee as such, much less a recognition of what the committee has meant in the evolution of human society.

There was a time -- and how necessary it is to remember its existence -- when committees inspired hope and confidence, when intelligent concerned men deeply engaged in the search for solutions to the critical problems of that day turned to the committee as to a veritable *deus ex machina*. The committee, which had been there all along though somewhat in the background, suddenly seemed capable of an infinite variety of uses, and it was not long before it had acquired all the relentless momentum of a fad. The European of early modern times might be forgiven for his enthusiasm for this toy. After all he came to the committee form with a freshness which has long since disappeared; he discovered committees before generations of use and abuse had dulled their charm. He could count himself lucky that a social group which had been known to primitive societies and antiquity had reappeared just at the moment when it was so desperately needed.[1] The demands placed on governments had increased by many magnitudes, and they could not possibly operate without the use of new mental categories, new administrative techniques, new institutional forms. The 'New Monarchies' quite as much as the new religious communities and the new commercial ventures required the contribution of committees if they were to get through their mounting official business. The inevitable drawbacks of the committee were not yet plain for all to see: no one had yet realized just how much valuable time would be wasted, how slow these bodies would be in coming to a decision, how much rhetoric would be expended for rhetoric's sake. What counted was the beneficial effects that outweighed the weaknesses: the importance and value of hearing a number of opinions on an issue, the wholesome diminishing of the influence and possible self-interest of one man, the greater degree of rationality and objectivity which permeated committee discussion.[2]

The committee, if it was far from having attained maturity or even the zenith of its power and influence, had entered upon a vigorous period of adolescence, and in the rush to confine political and social forces within its limits it was not too much to say that man, that *homo sapiens,* was in addition to all his other traits well on his way to being known as a committee-maker, a collegial animal. Europe in the fifteenth and sixteenth centuries already possessed a number of councils and advisory committees which often were informal and without any permanent organization or fixed personnel, and these councils proliferated with great ease as if to take advantage of the new fashion. Nothing could resist or cared to resist the universal sway of council, *conseil, consejo, consilio, Rat, Rad,* even Soviet.

To this further extension of a form that had already proven its usefulness there was now added the more revolutionary and significant development of the diffusion of the *collegium formatum,* a process that reached its peak in the seventeenth century. It was the committee in this specialized form that was in the long run to be the most productive addition to European public administration.[3] The *collegium formatum* transformed the advisory committee into an active and decision-making link in the administrative hierarchy. Where before there had been one officer of the Crown working with a few secretaries and assistants there now appeared a committee in his place, a committee that made its decisions most often on the basis of a majority vote. A number of top officials graded according to office and social distinction participated now in forming a policy, and if the sovereign retained full authority over these decisions he had to depend more and more on the fairly self-contained activity of a number of these *collegia.* Though the *collegia* were often thought of as a Swedish invention no nation or kingdom could claim a copyright. They were yet another impressive proof of the fact that a generalized need for more advanced techniques and forms had found some response in the *collegium formatum.*

These councils and *collegia* existed in rare profusion, as the forms were adapted to the particular needs and traditions of the various European states. Indeed, it was only a matter of time before a further nuance would be added to the work of the *collegia,* when a committee would appear that would coordinate the work of several such bodies so that they might work more closely and effectively in the common interest.[4] One such coordinating committee made its first appearance on the scene in Vienna during the winter of 1697.[5] Twice a week a small group of Austrian officials foregathered in a townhouse belonging to a member of the group. These were no run-of-the-mill bureaucrats toiling over a routine assignment, but the best that the Court of Vienna had to offer in the way of intelligence and experience. The committee was in fact composed of the chief advisers of Emperor Leopold I, men who happened to be in charge of the chief governmental agencies of the Austrian Monarchy. Their names, titles, and the official responsibilities which they had acquired testified to the fact that they had been called together on a matter of great importance. And surely this was the case. Action was desperately needed if the Emperor was to put his finances into something approaching order. Long years of war and the prospect of additional involvement in a great European conflict in the immediate future combined to push the Imperial Treasury to the point of bankruptcy. The Emperor and these men had been responsible for the more dynamic foreign policy that had been pursued in the wake of the defeat of the Turks before the gates of Vienna in 1683, but this leap into the dark so out of keeping with the customary timidity of the German Habsburgs had placed the ultimate degree of strain on the financial resources the Monarchy possessed. A sense of urgency presided over the committee meetings; only a crisis of such proportions could have led to such frequent meetings at a Court where not even impending disaster was allowed to break into the traditional round of pious practices and festivities.

In a formal sense the new committee had been charged with reorganizing the method of collecting the war-tax, the *contributio*. This reorganization was to be carried out by the apparently simple device of bringing the amount of the tax into line with the projected expenditures on the army. An assignment so narrowly conceived could not, however, fail to be the point of departure for a wide-ranging discussion on everything that had a bearing on military policy, the military budget, the political and constitutional framework of the government of the lands of the House of Austria. The members of the committee had to assume that even their limited authority carried with it the responsibility to think in terms of a reform no matter how partial and limited that might be. For any increase in the tax meant that the component parts of the Monarchy would become deeply and reluctantly involved, that what was under discussion in the meetings of their committee would have incalculable consequences for the conduct of the war against the Turks (already in its fourteenth year), the preparations for renewed war in the west, the relationship of the central government to the kingdoms, duchies and counties, the interaction of the various groups of society, the extent to which Austria under these pressures would have to embark upon a program of modernization or choose to remain behind in the general move towards modernity. In so broad a perspective the question of the appearance or non-appearance of a certain amount of gulden became so crucial for the life of the Monarchy that it could no longer be left to the generals, the Treasury officials, the tax collectors, to the local Estates (the *Stände*). Gulden were prosaic enough against the background of the continuing fete of the Austrian Baroque, but no one could any longer doubt that they constituted the political, financial, and military heart of the matter. They were the *nervus rerum gerendarum*, as the contemporaries chose to express it, the fulcrum on which all the work of government finally had to turn.

Most of the blame for this difficult and embarrassing state of affairs had to be laid at the door of the increased demands posed by late seventeenth century warfare. War had ceased to be something of a sport and a noble avocation and had become an industry that consumed most of the scant revenues then available to European monarchs and princes. Each state of any size had to maintain a large standing army, take note of the advances in weaponry and tactics, make room for the higher levels of training, discipline and control on the field of battle, and this meant ever larger expenditures. For the governmental offices and agencies that had arisen at an earlier time the changed conditions of warfare could only mean the ultimate test of their powers of survival. The lines which had customarily separated one office from another began to buckle and to break down under the pressure even though the officials appeared to believe that the old delimitations were still honored in practice. The isolation of offices and officials could no longer be tolerated as the problem deserted the military sphere and became so much involved in political and financial matters. All these men were finally involved in the pursuit of funds, and all began to lament their general inability to handle a situation that increasingly verged on organized chaos. Some years after the foundation of the new coordinating committee Eugene of Savoy, who was rather new to the confusion and impotence of the central administration, confessed how amazed he was by the state of affairs he had discovered:

> I can assure you that if I had not been present and had seen all of this with my own eyes no one could have made me believe it. For if the entire Monarchy was to be reduced to the ultimate extremity where it faced complete ruin and it could be saved by fifty thousand gulden or even less if produced in a hurry, one would simply have to let matters take their course and allow the disaster to take place.[6]

If there was to be any hoped for improvement in that winter of 1697 it would have to come about through the common effort and inspiration of four main agencies: the Austrian Court Chancellery (*Hofkanzlei*), the Court Treasury (*Hofkammer*), the Court War Council (*Hofkriegsrat*), and -- following very much behind -- the War Commissariat (*Kriegscommissariat*). These agencies were in large measure responsible for the main business of the central administration, particularly as it concerned the military budget. The first three had an imposing record of activity that extended far back in time, but past history showed little promise of assisting them now. Indeed, the very creativity which the Habsburgs had displayed in establishing these *collegia formata* in the first place might, if not watched very carefully, win for them the 'penalty for taking the lead.' The Treasury and the War Council had been impressive advances at the time of their creation, but they had been content to maintain themselves rather than to respond with greater sensitivity and flexibility to the increased demands of a radically different situation. Even that fount of all knowledge and decision, the Privy Council (*Geheimrat*) which also had been developed in the sixteenth century could not be of much assistance now. Its inmmense size and the pokiness of its movement had led to the creation of a small and more effective Privy Conference (*Geheime Konferenz*) in 1669.[7] But so great was the pressure even on that new council that it had begun to show signs of incipient decay and senility, when it had not even existed for thirty years. Was it any wonder, then, that Emperor Leopold turned in his growing desperation about finances to a new body, a committee that would be composed of the key men in the Chancellery, the Treasury, the War Council, and the War Commissariat?

Perhaps if these men and a few others thrown in for good measure could meet informally and frequently, they would be able to break through the false limits of their specialized functions and produce a program that his government so obviously lacked at the time. In taking such a decisive step the Emperor confounded momentarily at least those unsympathetic observers who complained about his lack of decision and his excessive reliance on the friendly offices of Divine Providence. In moments of crisis Leopold did incline to expect salvation from yet another 'miracle of the House of Austria,' but in calling this new committee into being he revealed an unexpected energy and reliance on purely natural forces.

In the official Instructions which established this committee it received the sonorous name of *the Deputatio des Status Publico-oeconomico-militaris* (Ad Hoc Committee on the Military Budget).[8] In an age given to such sesquipedalian nomenclature such a name deserved some pride of place. In addition it had the merit of pointing up the three dimensions -- political, financial, and military -- in which any discussion of the military budget had to take place. It also invoked the traditional '*Deputatio*,' the practice of setting aside small groups to handle specific questions. As early as the beginning of the century the moody and retiring Rudolf II had had the custom of deputizing a few of his councillors to represent him in his absence. This practice soon grew to include the setting up of ad hoc subcommittees of the Privy Council to consider questions that could not be easily handled by the Privy Council as a whole. The term *Deputatio* had embarked on a long and not entirely dishonorable career, and while few specific cases of its use as an administrative device were destined to make a name for themselves it came to be a proven method of concentrating attention on a specific problem when all else had failed. Leopold frequently made use of such deputations, and his recourse to the name and the activity which it represented in this instance was at once a sign of the emergency and the view of a deputation as a last resort. The term '*Status*' could claim an even more venerable usage. In this instance, however, an exact modern equivalent is hard to find. It probably should be equated with the military budget (witness the German usage of *Etat*) even though nothing quite as formal and as organized as a budget existed at the time. But any treatment of the political and financial aspects of the military establishment could mean little else than a consideration of the ways and means that would be required for the maintenance of a large and permanent military establishment.[9]

In the course of the Deputation's career its ponderous official name fell into disuse, and those who were familiar with its work at all chose to give it a nickname by calling it either the *Mittelsdeputation* (Ministerial Ad Hoc Committee) or *Stadtdeputation* (City committee).[10] *Hofmittel* was the term then in official use for any central agency of the Austrian government, and the nickname made it abundantly clear that this ad hoc committee was not a subcommittee of the Privy Conference but a committee composed of the governmental agencies.[11] The use of the word 'deputation' would never entirely overlook the fact that it had originally meant a small ad hoc group; it was to be one of the contributions of the new Deputation to give the word the meaning of a committee specifically concerned with the financial problems arising out of war.

Once beyond the tremulous moment of its founding and baptism the Deputation displayed an impressive amount of activity, and for a time it gave promise of being the answer to the Emperor's high expectations of its work. But his own indecisiveness, the changes in the Deputation's personnel, the insurmountable obstacles it encountered along the way caused it to be reduced and in a relatively brief period of time to a shadow of its former self. All vigor gone and all official enthusiasm long since frittered away the Deputation did not have the good taste to die. It lingered uncertainly on the margins of governmental activity more chorus now than an active participant in those affairs. It continued to exist and that was a triumph of a kind. In 1704 it still could be discussed in a plan for a general reform of the central administration. In 1705 it still could issue orders to the Hungarian administration at Bratislava. In 1711 Count Johann Wenzel Wratislaw referred to the work of the Deputation as to one of the chief standing committees concerned with the public business of the Austrian

Monarchy, when he explained its procedures in a letter to the new Emperor Charles VI.[12]

In the course of Charles' reign the Deputation made even less of an impression on contemporary observers but that it continued to exist much transformed and attenuated cannot be questioned at all. Indeed, it required the healthy sweeping out of old forms connected with the great reform program of Maria Theresa and Count Haugwitz to finish it off for good, as what was left of its official business was turned over to a newly-established *Conferentia in internis* in 1749.[13]

Our Deputation perished in rather good company, it must be admitted, but there was precious little time in the excitement of new directions to devote any attention to obsequies for defunct deputations and committees. For the better part of its career it had persisted in a state of suspended animation, an old administrative device that might at any time be revived or, on the other hand, be abolished for good. This political limbo to which it had been assigned meant that it aroused little interest in the world at large, not to mention the official world of Austrian adminstration. Perhaps the nature of its business played some part in that none too salutary neglect: however important the military budget might be in fact, discussions about it were not likely to titillate a general audience which much preferred dynastic marriages, battles, and great official festivities. Austria's increasingly important role in European affairs attracted a good deal of attention that might have embraced the existence of and the work of something like the Deputation. But success had been denied to it, and this fatal flaw in its history and composition could never be forgotten or overlooked!

Yet it had sufficient power of survival (and what Austrian could deny this some measure of respect?) to last fifty years and to engage in the very passing interest of historians generations after its official unlamented demise. When it did emerge once more it depended for what reputation it might possess on the interests, the biases, the archival discoveries of a small elite group of Austrian historians whose course of scholarship brought them upon the vestiges the Deputation had left behind. Hermann Bidermann mentioned it and not in passing though not exactly in an entirely accurate way when he set out to follow the growth of that centripetal principle in the life of the Austrian Monarchy, the *Gesammtstaatsidee*. For him the Deputation and its work could be taken as a sign of the expectation that all the parts of the Monarchy, Hungary included, were expected to do their share in maintaining the central government. But he was searching for more formidable proof of his thesis, and his glance at the Deputation was a brief and superficial one.[14] The Deputation had to wait another generation until Freiherr von Mensi published his classic treatment of Austrian finances in the first forty years of the eighteenth century to receive the kind of response informed and appreciative that it deserved.[15] Thanks to Mensi the Deputation won a place in the first volumes of that history of the Austrian central administration that is one of the chief embellishments of Austrian historiography. Thomas Fellner, who was responsible for the initial volumes in the series, devoted a section of his general discussion of the beginnings of that administration to be found in the chapter *"Der geheime Rat, die Konferenz und die Deputation."* The chief merit of his work was to bring together all of the information that was then available in one place and to add to this the publication of the *Instructio* that set down the ground rules for the work of the Deputation.[16]

For all this absolutely necessary introduction to the problem of the Deputation the degree of interest it elicited still did not go much beyond the natural limits of polite awareness and curiosity. The first wave of references to its existence and work produced little or no echo in the handbooks and the classic general histories of Austria and of Hungary that have been produced in the course of this century. The very things that had excited the interest of contemporaries to the detriment of the reputation of efforts to manage the military budget also operated at a great distance in time. Foreign affairs, military campaigns, the high moments of Austrian Baroque culture consumed all space and interest. Little or no energy remained for a subject that had so little to recommend it as a consolation in adversity or as a claim to Austrian greatness. The eventual appearance of a monograph could not be discounted, but it began to look increasingly likely that the brief renaissance in Deputation studies which had taken place between 1867 and 1907 had ended for good. The Deputation appeared to be settled in as comfortably as it could to the special niche reserved for it in that cabinet of natural curiosities, noble administrative experiments that have been tried and have failed and whose sole appeal is to the antiquarian or the entomologist of administrative species and genera.

This might have been the end of the story if the Deputation had not prepared a pleasant surprise for one visitor at least to the extraordinarily rich collections of the *Haus-, Hof- und Staatsarchiv* in Vienna.[17] For by some magic best known to itself the Deputation had managed to preserve a series of the protocols of its meetings in the early years of its existence. Though this collection was small in size there could be no doubt that it is one of the most precious indicators we possess of the inner workings of a committee at the end of the seventeenth century. Though it may appear to be the very height of 'Habsburg imperialism' to linger on this point, an argument can surely be made for the value of the collection on the grounds that it is so detailed and that it manages to give an extremely accurate picture of what went on at the meetings. Other committees, councils, and commissions in Austria as well as in the rest of Europe may well have had greater importance for the course of European history, but they made startlingly little provision for their afterlife. Some did not bother to keep records at all, and those that did consigned them to the flames or to the oblivion of country houses where they have perished or have been lost altogether from sight. And even where such sources do exist they fail to attain to the degree of 'living presence' presented by the deputation protocols. The miracle that permitted this committee to preserve its identity and its activity against all the ravages of more than two centuries makes it possible now to remove it from that cabinet of natural curiosities and to make it the subject of an extensive study of Austrian government and politics in the period of its initial activity. The secret is out quite obviously, and the chief ministers of Emperor Leopold I now run the risk of being overheard, of being subjected to the far from tender mercies of that professional eavesdropper, the historian. If they knew what might have been made of their deliberations by the secretary with his consummately appraising eye and what might in time be made of those notations they would have been less unguarded in what they said. Thanks to their aristocratic insouciance, to the energy of the secretary, and to the good fortune that preserves these pages for so long a time the Deputation can now manage to exist on its own feet and more than that to become the focus of larger perspectives not all of which have to do with the work of the Deputation in a narrow sense.

One obviously has to begin with the biography of the committee, with the chronicle of its activity in its golden age, roughly from 1697 to the death of Leopold I. The creator of the Deputation is the first object of attention and then the agencies, the parties, the political traditions which made up the context in which it operated. More specifically its own marching orders come into discussion, the membership, the kind of reporting it received, the actual history of the meetings, and last but not least the extent to which it had influence on a specific area of concern, the war-tax as it was levied on the Kingdom of St. Stephen. But even this is only a beginning, for chronicle, biographical miniatures, explications of ancient texts do not exhaust the work of the historian nor the rich possibilities that adhere to these protocols.

High on the list of priorities one expects to find here the chance to take a good close look at the Austrian system of government and the chief figures involved in it at the end of the seventeenth century. Though these men have been mentioned in most available accounts and have even attracted sufficient attention to justify brief biographies or articles in biographical dictionaries they generally lack that fleshed out appearance that is encountered in their opposite numbers in Paris, London, and The Hague. Perhaps they were partially responsible for this. As individuals and as a group they were not sufficiently impressive to require study in depth. But it may be that their skeletal appearance has not a little to do with the milieu in which they operated which was notoriously not given to self-analysis and to the kind of reflection that produced long diaries and interesting correspondence. Letters and diaries exist, and some have even been published, but the results rarely seem worth the work involved, for as works of revelation of spiritual interiors, of the 'inner space' of important men at the Court of Vienna they leave almost everything unanswered, unsaid. Revelation if it came at all came in the form of their style of life and style of dying, their great houses in the city and their castles in the country. But as for the views they cherished and the methods they followed, their general perspective on the world the protocols of the Deputation do not fail to say many interesting and suggestive things.

These men were largely drawm from the same generation, a distinction which they shared with the Emperor himself. They were old men approaching the end of their official life and of life itself when they entered upon this new responsibility. Their productive years, their heroic years were behind them, and they faced the newer problems with a trepidation that comes through clearly in the most banal statement of an opinion. At the very conclusion of their work they paused momentarily in these conversations to provide themselves with a memorial and to make sense as best they could out of the efforts they had made in the service of the House of Austria.

Men drawn from one generation, the members of the Deputatio were for the most part men of one social stratum or *Stand.* In their case they were well-established members of the great and cosmopolitan Habsburg aristocracy. They stood at the very peak of the society in which they lived, yielding place of honor only to the members of the dynasty. As great landed magnates they found themselves condemned to playing a double role as advisers of the Emperor and as leaders in organized opinion in the country. They served in Vienna, and they were deeply involved in the local Stände if only because they had estates to think about, sons to find offices for, daughters to marry, and a position to maintain that was a family responsibility. This gave these men an air of uncertainty, of second thoughts and hesitations that were not expressed with any clarity. In Vienna they were committed to preserving the central authority which could only mean the extension of its influence; at the local level they were committed to the defense of rights and privileges, of noble liberties and regional and social egoisms. Cosmopolitan in style and in origin, these magnates managed to retain a provincial attachment that was often the product of only a generation or two of immersion in the Austrian or Bohemian countryside. The protocols give us some idea of how they went about the business of reconciling what we take to be contradictory loyalties, and we discover without surprise that the resulting amalgam was more complex and rich in signification than one might have been led to expect.

The protocols reveal these men hard at work on a definite problem that was of sufficient importance to arouse their personal involvement at the deepest level. Though they did not realize that they were engaged in decision-making they were in fact doing just that, and this degree of unawareness makes their approach all the more exciting for the sociologist and the student of public administration. Here the whole process can be followed from beginning to end, from the definition of the problem to its attempted solution. The members of the Deputation were not operating with more recent categories in mind, and for that very reason their activity helps to raise questions about some of the more commonly accepted ones: 'Habsburg absolutism' for example.[18] The term has a pleasant ring to it and has managed for a number of good reasons to achieve wide acceptance from the experts. But if it is to continue to be used it may not be too much to say that it will have to reckon with these protocols and these meetings for the light they shed on what official practice happened to be at a time when 'Habsburg absolutism' appears to have been in full flower. The Anglo-Saxon mind may be forgiven for its immediate reluctance to accept the instant they begin to assume a life and a momentum of their own. But if it can be established on the basis of a case study which uses the Deputation that 'Habsburg absolutism' answers a definite historiographical need, then its place among the conventional signs and symbols of the historical interpretation of the Habsburg Monarchy in the seventeenth century would be assured.

In the course of determining the validity of 'Habsburg absolutism' it is also possible to examine the arguments for the use of political party as a meaningful term. 'Ideology' is too strong a word and too anachronistic in this context to describe what these men felt about the political process in its ends and means, but there is sufficient evidence in the protocols to suggest that the political groups that existed were not mere clusters of personalities or cliques built on a shared interest. The history of the internal politics of the Court of Vienna has too often been written in the manner of a *chronique scandaleuse*. It is high time to begin to wonder at least if factors at once more basic and perhaps less piquant were not operating here -- even in the reign of Leopold I.

Up to this point the protocols have served as a vehicle for re-examining a number of conventional assessments of Austrian politics and society. But a careful reading may well raise questions that are greater in scope and in ultimate significance than those already mentioned. There comes a moment when the analysis of the protocols demands techniques not unlike those available to the biblical exegete in the science of hermeneutics. For this is nothing more or less than a systematic effort to isolate a set of basic principles to guide the exegete in understanding the Sacred Scriptures. A source as secular in character and in content as these protocols may look out of place in such a context, but the more one thinks about it the more it demands an analysis that will transliterate its statements into a modern idiom.[19]

For each society has its unique structure and its unique form of communication, and much of the meaning it tried to convey is lost until this translation not just of words and sentences but of a whole discourse takes place. Patterns existed in the discourse of the Austrians at the end of the seventeenth century that were visible in the social structure and in the language they used to convey what they meant by God, Emperor, Church, and even Deputation. It does have to be admitted that these Austrians communicated to a substantial degree by the use of non-verbal signs and symbols that cannot be found in any protocols and that the full meaning of the work of the Deputation could be discovered only by knowing many things -- the gestures, the pecking order of the members, the costume, the intonations of speech -- that are forever lost. But what survives may well be enough to isolate and to describe the collective mentality at the base of those discussions.

Distinguished scholars who have studied this period in Austrian history have already described this mentality with varying degrees of success. Some of their descriptions have become virtually canonical: 'Baroque,' 'aristocratic ethos,' and the 'Austrian genius' are some of the more memorable ones.[20] What has happened is that terms drawn from different levels of abstraction -- artistic style, style of life, national spirit -- have been used to express the uniqueness of the Austrian mentality. Perhaps the protocols are not the obvious place to look for more clues; they are not sufficiently self-conscious or literary to sustain a highly conceptualized form of inquiry. But they are there all the same, and as a far from mute testimony as to the perspectives and values of Austria *circa* 1700 they must not be overlooked. The use that will be made of them here in the quest for the collective mentality can only be a step in the right direction. It would require the work of a great many scholars in as many fields to produce the kind of results that would be at all satisfactory. But since there is little likelihood of a sudden explosion of Austrian Baroque studies the reflections to be found here will have to suffice for the moment.

The Deputation through its protocols tells us far more than the story of one committee among thousands of others. It raises substantial questions about the significance of personalities, institutions, and events in Austrian history, and in so doing directs attention to similar committees elsewhere in Europe. Austrian history carries with it no guaranteed claim to splendid isolation, and the experience of the Deputation calls into question the experience of other committees that bear a family resemblance. The Austrian coordinating committee that struggled so valiantly with the practical problems raised by war, finance, taxation and reform was after all but one facet in a larger picture -- the contribution of the committees and the *collegia* to European history. When the history of that contribution is written (and it, too, will require the work of many scholars and many disciplines), the Deputation may expect to find its rightful place at last. A learned footnote will then serve the purpose of meting out the exact amount of remembrance and recognition it should receive.

Notes

1. For a typically brilliant and long-range view that combines history
and typology, cf. Max Weber, *Wirtschaft und Gesellschaft* (Tübingen, 1924), 159 ff.

2. F. Hartung; R. Mousnièr, Quelques problèmes concernant la monarchie absolue," X
Congresso Internazionale di *Scienze Storicàe, Relazioni*, IV, 29.

3. Gustav Schmoller discusses the *collegium formatum* at some length in his
introduction to *Die Behördenorganisation und die allgemeine Staatsverwaltung
Preussens im 18. Jahrhundert* (Acta Borussica: Denkmäler der Preussisohen
Staatsverwaltung im 18. Jahrhundert) (Berlin, 1894), Bd. I, 59-67.

4. Pol Meyer, *Administrative Organization: A Comparative Study of Public
Administration* (London, 1957). Scattered through this book are a number of important
comments on collegiality and coordinating committees.

5. Thomas Fellner; Heinrich Kretschmayr, *Die Österreichische Zentralverwaltung*
(Veröffentlichungen der Kommission für Neuere Geschichte
Österreichs, 5) (Vienna, 1907), Abt. I, Bd. I, 56.

6. A. von Arneth, *Prinz Eugen von Savoyen* (Vienna, 1864), I, 212, quoting a letter
from Eugene to Guido von Starhemberg, Vienna, Oct. 3, 1703. This process has been
carefully studied by Henry F. Schwarz in his *Imperial Privy Council in the Seventeenth
Century* (Harvard Historical Studies, LIII) (Cambridge, Mass., 1943).

8. The *Instruktion* has been published in Fellner-Kretschmayr, *op. cit.*,
Abt. I. Bd. III, 24-38.

9. C. du Fresne D. du Cange, *Glossarium mediae et infime Latinitatis* (Niort, 1886),
VII, 590.

10. The question of nomenclature is a most complicated one, and little can be said that
is entirely convincing. For some idea of the confusion of terms, cf. Fellner-
Kretschmayr, *op. cit.*, Abt. I, Bd. I, 62-63.

11. *Ibid.*, 63n.

12. Cf. "Denkschriften uber den Zustand der Zentralbehorden und a. h. Resolution
Kaiser Josefs I. daruber. 1704-1706." Fellner-Kretschmayr, *op. cit.*, Abt. I. Bd. III, 40-
48; Wratislaw to Emperor Charles VI, Vienna, March 27, 1711, "Korrespondenz mit
König Karl III. von Spanien," *Mitteilungen des Instituts für österreichische
Geschichtsforschung*, Bd. 16, 88.

13. Fellner-Kretschmayr, *op. cit.*, Abt. I, Bd. I, 63.

14. H. I. Bidermann, *Geschichte der österreichischen Gesammt-Staats-Idee* 1526-1804 (Innsbruck, 1867),Abt. I, 39-42.

15. Franz Freiherrn v. Mensi. *Die Finanzen Österreichs von 1701 bis 1740* (Wien, 1890), 80 ff.

16. Fellner-Kretschmayr, *op. cit.*, Abt. I, Bd. I, 37-67.

17. The protocols are a part of the larger collection of *Vorträge*.
For details see below.

18. W. B. Slottman, "The Emperor's New Clothes: The Nature of Habsburg Absolutism," an unpublished paper delivered at the Far Western Slavic Conference, Berkeley, Calif., May 12, 1966.

19. The work of Heidegger and Gadamer in this field is well known. I have found two articles in the collection *New Theology No. 4*, ed. Martin E. Marty and Dean G. Peerman (New York, 1967) particularly stimulating: Mircea Eliade, "Crisis and Renewal in History of Religions," pp. 19-38, and Heinrich Ott, "Language and Understanding," pp. 124-146. Heidegger treatment of the figure of Abraham and Sancta Clara, a preacher at the Court of Vienna in Leopold I's time is a spur to additional work along this line, cf. "Über Abraham a Sancta Clara: Ansprache zu einem Schulfest," *Wort and Wahrheit* (XXII), Nr. 7, 437-442.

20. In this connection I have in mind particularly the work of Otto
Brunner, Robert Kann, and Carl Schorske. Brunner discusses the aristocratic ethos in his epoch-making book *Adeliges Landleben und europaischer Geist* (Salzburg, 1949), 61-138. Kann discusses the Baroque concept at the beginning of his *A Study in Austrian Intellectual History: From Late Baroque to Romanticism* (New York, 1960), 1-4, and focuses upon its contradictions; later on he makes reference to "...specific characteristics of the Austrian people, what might be termed their specific genius, (which) gave it its peculiar character," ibid., 48. Carl Schorske frequently refers to 'Austrian aristocratic culture' in his work; he rightly emphasizes its aesthetic components and Catholic cultural influences. Cf. for example, "Politics and the Psyche in Fin de Siecle Vienna; Schnitzler and Hofmennsthal," *American Historical Review* (LXVI), #4, July, 1961, 933-934.

Chapter One
Coram Caesare / Final Authority

"*Sei Kaiser und kein Musikant,*
sei Kaiser und kein Jäger,
sei Kaiser und kein Jesuit."
- Contemporary pamphlet

A Phanariote Greek in the Turkish diplomatic service who had come to Austria on a peace mission and had been detained there for many months thought to win some concessions for his party by paying a pretty compliment to Emperor Leopold I. He did this by comparing His Most August Imperial Majesty to a sun, a sun resplendent with every adorable and royal virtue.[1] The figure he chose was a singularly appropriate one, for it set off a most elaborate chain of images and associations. The business of comparing emperors with the sun was as old as recorded history, and the Roman emperors, the object of so much heavyhanded German mimicry, had made a special practice of using the sun image. Their distant 'descendants' in Germany had not been averse to copying them in this instance; the Habsburg Charles V had gone so far as to state as a positive fact on his coinage: "*Quod in coelis sol, hoc in terra Caesar est.*" [2] Caesar was the center of a system, a cosmos, in his case of a world-empire, the first world-empire upon which the sun obligingly enough never set.

Leopold might with somewhat less assurance make a similar claim. After all the Holy Roman Emperor remained the chief temporal figure in what was left of Christendom. Tradition as well as figures of speech reinforced this view, though it was perfectly clear that his thrusting relative in France Louis XIV would compete with him for the title by encouraging the belief that he was the Sun-King, the *roi soleil.*

The French solar system looked too new, and though it was assuredly a marvel of simplicity when compared with Leopold's rather pre-Copernican cosmos it failed to be entirely convincing. Leopold's place at the center had the ratification of custom, and the system itself wore a more familiar even patriarchal air. Its planets and moons moved about their sun with a most Ptolemaic convolution. They derived their movement from the center, and, at the same time, received these solar impulses in their own customary, that is highly selective way. Inferior bodies that they were, they had not yet resigned themselves to the simple task of revolving in their orbits without occasional variations and departures from the norm. Yet not for a moment was it possible for them to imagine themselves without the *sol*, without Caesar, even when Caesar happened to be represented by the not exactly overpowering Leopold I. First impressions were not critical here; the force of custom and the system's inherent order of authority were. They needed their *sol* and needed him perhaps with a greater degree of conviction than was possible elsewhere. In the lands of the House of Austria the Emperor did more than preside at the top of the social pyramid and direct the business of government, here he and he alone provided the state's *raison d'être*; he welded that curious collection of historical and geographical personalities into something approaching an entity of its own. The remark about Leopold being like a sun idly tossed off by Alexander Mavrokordatos might be considered a most apposite way of describing the nature and the general outlines of the Austrian political and social system.

What manner of man was this who had been called by God and heredity to such a demanding assignment, to such a crucial role in European affairs? A first glance did not suggest that Leopold was a promising object for compliments no matter how traditional they might be. He had none of that dramatic self-assertion and calculation of his cousin Louis, and his kingship, though it was always present, did not incarnate itself by design in every word and gesture. Dignity he possessed, but his was a dignity of such long standing that those who possessed it seemed unconscious that it was theirs by birth. Leopold felt no desperate need to impose himself on his visitors by personal charm, brilliance of costume or immediacy of charisma; he expected that visitors would be so sensitized by ritual and historical association that they would realize without needing to be reminded of the fact that the very mortal man before them, physically unattractive and shabbily dressed, with a tendency to be melancholy and to be content with commonplaces, that this man in whose lip, underslung jaw, and face the Habsburg family traits were unforgettably displayed, was no less than Imperial Majesty, the chief temporal representative of God Himself.

The effect of that presence could quickly disappear at the slightest contact with reality, and Leopold viewed from a distance lost much of his power to engage men's minds and emotions. Louis XIV drew much of the attention to himself, while Leopold, the backward country cousin, found himself consigned to a less important place in the annals of European history. The official Court Historiographers who devoted so many pages and such flattering titles to 'Leopold the Great' could not hide the fact that they found him to be alarmingly devoid of the *virtú* that characterized every great statesman, general, or diplomat.[3] In the absence of a Saint-Simon whose literary gift and love-hate had immortalized a Louis XIV, Leopold had to depend for what reputation he might secure on the Venetian Ambassadors, the stray diplomat with an eye for character portrayal, the memoirist who tried his hand at providing a fresh and breezy account of the Court of Vienna.

What had happened to the Venetians? In the presence of this Emperor, their political realism, their unfailing sense of what was important and what was unimportant apparently failed them. They could produce nothing more than a string of flattering commonplaces, as if by that device to confess their impotence and to warn those who might give too much credence to what they said. Much that was positive in their portraits of Leopold did have reference to his virtues as a man rather than as a ruler, but anyone reading these despatches and final relations in Venice must have been encouraged to read between the lines in order to extract any residue of political analysis. Perhaps Venice was already beginning to experience its decline, and its best diplomats only gave proof of that in what they had to say about their great neighbor to the north. Perhaps the Venetian diplomats were struggling to comprehend how so unheroic a man as Leopold I managed to rule Austria when it had attained to its most heroic and victorious stance.[4]

The French and English envoys were less verbose and less inclined to overlook the shadows in Leopold 's character and career.[5] Much that transpired in Vienna did not fail to puzzle them and annoy them, these men of the great world, but even their priceless self-confidence appeared shaken after they had attempted to describe the Emperor. As for the memoirists they were on firmer ground precisely because they felt no responsibility for transmitting political intelligence. They made the most of gossip and the occasional glimpses they had of the Court. The fact that these men, as foreigners, could hardly grasp the significance of much of what they saw did not depress the Viennese. After all, Leopold's capital had a long history of encouraging tourists to mistake appearance for reality.[6]

Historians who have followed in the wake of these men have attempted to improve on the very mixed picture of Leopold that is to be found in such sources. After several generations a conventional picture has emerged that has shown remarkable promise as the final considered verdict on Leopold I as Emperor and as human being.[7] Indeed, Heinrich Ritter von Srbik was moved not so many years ago to express his belief that it is possible now to capture the very essence of Leopold and in 'clear and simple lines,' freed at long last from the imperfections introduced by past historians.[8]

In the hands of such an acknowledged master of the craft we may well encounter a portrait of Leopold done from life, though the nagging suspicions remains that Srbik, for all his undoubted learning and sensitivity, has probably been guilty of a venial sin of historiographical hubris in making such a claim. Even an epistemology based on common sense would cast doubt on the ability of even the most gifted to capture the 'essence' of another individual, and when the act of knowing is complicated by distance in time the prospect seems even more remote. The situation is reminiscent of those advisers of Leopold who imagined that they could control him pretty much according to their own whims. Prince Wenzel Lobkowitz, who came as close as any man to doing just that, even went so far as to express the opinion that the Emperor was like a "statue that could be moved from place to place at will." [9]   Doubtless he had occasion to remember so mistaken a view while he vegetated on his estates a few years later, a chief minister no longer and banished from the Imperial Court.

The temptation is strong, then, to reproduce the conventional picture with a few minor modifications.   Prudence at least would suggest such a course.   But the fact that Leopold played so critical a role in the life of the Deputation makes it all the more necessary to be imprudent for once by attempting something that is wellnigh impossible: the character analysis of the man who created the Deputation and who, while it continued to operate, acted as its final court of appeal.

Behind the elaborate facade which ceremonial and custom had created, there was first and foremost a man who possessed a well-defined set of personal traits.   Too often these have been listed without any connecting link between them with the result that Leopold has seemed to be more contradictory than he may well have been in fact. Without some principle of explanation these traits persist in a state of confusion, and the significance of much of what he did remains lost from view.

His contemporaries experienced the need to classify the Emperor by the use of categories, typologies, that were available to them at the time.   His German biographer Gottlieb Rinck set Leopold against the background of the three passions which he felt to be critical in the makeup of any human being: pride, pleasure, and avarice. Pride in the form of ambition dominated in his case with pleasure coming far behind (the Emperor's self-control was proverbial) and avarice playing little or no role at all. Apparently the phlegmatic humor dampened two of the passions and led to the possibility that Leopold might be described in a quick and summary way as phlegmatic. Rinck's scheme had all the virtues of a summary court martial: the judgment came quickly and decisively and without any effort to go much below the surface. [10] But the need for a scheme had been demonstrated beyond a doubt.

George Stepney, another contemporary of the Emperor, tried his luck in the following way:

> But as His Imperial Majesty is observed to be of an irresolute wavering temper,
> on which the last impressions ever make the deepest marks, this occasions that
> he is frequently torn several ways by the different inclinations of His ministers,
> who in a manner governed him by turns as if each commanded *de jour* (to which
> may be attributed those delays which have ever been too visible in all the designs
> and enterprises at the Imperial Court).[11]

Stepney went a bit deeper and, in so doing, hit upon what he took to be the key to Leopold's character -- his "irresolute wavering temper." It was striking, too, how he pointed up the degree to which impressions, particularly the most recent, influenced Leopold's views and the decisions that came only after such long delays.

Encouraged by such contemporary efforts and well aware of the fragility of such analysis one begins at the beginning -- in this instance at the level of external appearances. However deceiving they may be as a guide to a soul, they often hint at internal processes and mechanisms which are only imperfectly hidden from the public eye. Surely, this was true of Leopold. Short in height and not at all impressive in size, he possessed a good color and a fine head of hair. His expression was one of benevolence, and those who looked closely at his eyes imagined that they discovered a quiet dignity there. He spoke well and in a fine array of languages, indeed he might be counted something of a polyglot with all of the major European languages and some of the minor ones within his range. But it was difficult to place too much confidence in what he said, since so much of it was calculated to charm the visitor rather than to convey any hint of policy. He spoke so quietly as to be often inaudible, and whether this was from accident or design remained a question. His whole expression, dominated though it was by that unforgettable genetic imprint, tended to be serious. It was reported of him that he rarely smiled. His movements were uncertain and hesitant. The Most August Imperial Majesty had trouble in knowing what to do with his hat (the official etiquette helped out by allowing him to remain covered much of the time), his hands, his limbs. When he walked he acted as though he were about to fall, as if he were afraid that his next step might make him an object of the laughter of even his most loyal and devoted courtiers.[12]

In those appearances one can, if one has the desire to do so, recognize a character type that would achieve a degree of individuation depending on his circumstances, background, and experience. Leopold represented the kind of person whose affective life runs far behind his ability to express it in an external and active way.[13] There was nothing underdeveloped about his intelligence. He could and often did make impressive analyses of the political situation that extended to equally impressive notions of what had to be done about them. But diagnosis here had no complement in the actual power to cure. The fatal break between intelligence and volition made it impossible for him to act as he would have wished. He came to depend on others even when they were not as perceptive, because he did not trust his own judgment, because he could not imagine that he would ever be able to break through to the kind of concerted and dramatic action that his government needed so badly. When the situation grew desperate, he was often forced to make a decision, but even when a decision had been made after great delay and without any conviction that it was the right one, it required only "a tiny grain of sand" to prevent it from being carried through.[14]

Defeated so often in his attempts to establish a working relationship with the world of action and with events, Leopold developed a number of surrogates for action that encouraged him in the belief that he was fulfilling his obligations after all. These surrogates or stratagems took on a wide variety of forms and gave his personality the richness it surely possessed. There was his evident interest in the arts, for example. He loved literature, drama, and music. So far as the last was concerned he could claim to be a musician; he played several instruments, conducted orchestras, and even composed music. His poetic gift extended to the creation of Latin couplets which were often humorous and directed at contemporaries -- Louis XIV among them.[15] This artistic range and involvement was more than the usual round of festivities which formed a colorful background at any court. For Leopold the arts were not mere diversion and a surcease from official duty, but a chance to reveal gifts that could not be exposed to the harsh light of politics. Only in the realm of fantasy or in a dimension where the reality of the world about him had so little to say, did he feel entirely at home and confident of his own powers.

The escape, if one can call it that, into beauty was not the only escape route open to him. The family had developed a reputation for hunting that even then verged on the pathological. Endless hours were spent on the chase but what was distressing was the hecatombs of wild beasts these hunts produced.[16] Leopold was no exception, but here again a diversion that was common to all monarchs and aristocrats was not without the added significance of a refusal to face up to the need for the making and execution of wise policies. Gambling, too, though in a lesser degree, provided a mixture of diversion, and that mimicry of real situations that is said to play so important a role in the psycological makeup of the professional gambler. A sudden stroke of good luck was what the Emperor sought at the gambling tables, and this was virtually the same thing he sought in politics.

There was the escape, too, to be found in sheer drudgery and the immersion in trivia. In one year Leopold managed to write 386 letters, read and sign 8,625 official documents, and grant 481 audiences.[18] The very fact that a count was kept reveals how necessary it was to establish a record, as if all that work could be any substitute for political leadership. There was an additional story, too, connected with his handwriting. Like so much else about the man, it made little concession to the man who was not familiar with its eccentricities, its canonized forms of mystification. Special experts on his hand had to be employed to translate it for those who could easily admit that for them the writing of the Emperor was entirely illegible.

The most precious of all diversions for Leopold was his deep religious faith. His character type impelled him to some extent to religious feeling, and he was naturally adapted to that sensitivity to the supernatural that is so characteristic of religious experience. Though he has often been accused of mere superstition, of bigotry, of an excessive reliance on confessors and priests, of a piety that was somehow unmanly, there can be no doubt at all that his religion had profound roots and that he went far beyond the institutional forms available to him at the time.[19] If his piety was that of the House of Austria for the most part, the *pietas Austriaca*, a network of pious practices that had become virtually traditional, he had great faith in God and in the power of prayer.[20]   The trouble was that his uncertainty in the face of events encouraged him to adopt a religious passivity, a quietism in fact if not in theory, that verged on a magical notion of Divine Providence.[21]   God's will would be done, he could not doubt that, but God's will was inextricably connected with his own political deficiencies and with the safety and well-being of the House of Austria.   The 'miracle of the House of Austria' that had been taken to mean the sudden and inexplicable rescue from disaster.   In Leopold's mind this rare intervention of the supernatural had been devalued to the level of an almost daily occurrence. Saint Ignatius who bad encouraged his sons to pray as if everything depended on God and to work as if everything depended on their efforts would have been disappointed to see how little this splendidly Ignatian doctrine meant to Leopold, whose religious life had been formed to such a great extent by Jesuit teachers and confessors. His religion was not simply the religious reflection of his character type, but there could be no denying how much there was of his fatal flaw in his religious behavior.

There were compensations, perhaps even political ones, for his "irresolute wavering temper." He had a very rich emotional life as can be seen from his strong family ties and his positive gift for friendship. The devoted husband of three wives in succession, and a loving father of two future emperors and a bevy of Leopoldinian archduchesses, he aroused no hint of scandal at all in an age that considered scandal a political necessity. He made friends easily in his early years and only the suspicions automatically generated by his official role prevented him from doing so later on. His loyalty to these friends and to those who served him in any capacity was striking and an ironic comment on the equally ironic phrase *Dank vom Haus Habsburg.* Friends were all too quickly called upon to assume official positions and even when their good nature and charm proved hopelessly inadequate for their tasks, Leopold refused to dismiss them. He enjoyed having them about, and it was so infernally difficult to tell them that they had outlived their usefulness.[22]

However useful it may be to understand Leopold as a man with a set of traits that finds its explication finally in the "irresolute wavering temper" it would be a mistake to believe that this could be the whole story. For in addition to a character type Leopold also bore with him the marks of a long family tradition and of an extremely varied and lengthy personal experience.

The mere accident of birth had made him a Habsburg and a very special kind of Habsburg, those few individuals who collectively formed the last of the original male line. These *Althabsburger*, as they are usually called, carried many family traits and family traditions to an excess (was not this evident in their physiognomy?) that prefigured the end of the race.[23] Generations of intermarriage within the family had led to a situation that was not too far removed from the inbreeding of the Ptolemies, and the specialist in genealogy has a field day when he even begins to contemplate Leopold's place in the family tree. His sister Marianna had gone to Spain to become the second wife of Philip IV. Their daughter Margareta, the Inl'anta of so many portrait studies of Velasquez, had come to Vienna to become Leopold's first wife. But this was only the beginning of the ties which existed and which had probably begun to take their toll on the ability of the Habsburgs to reproduce themselves. The fear of extinction and the terrible consequences that would have for Austria and for Spain made the desperate quest for the Spanish inheritance something more than mere dynastic politics. Leopold himself had had to wait until 1678 for a viable male heir, the Archduke Joseph, and this long-awaited son was presented to him by his third wife.

The Habsburgs have such a long history as a European dynasty that they leave the door open to attempts to classify Habsburgs according to certain types. There were the dreamers, visionaries whose means never even began to approach their political aims -- Rudolf IV, Maximilian I, Rudolf II. There were the eminently practical and successful Habsburgs who managed to combine sufficient vision with an equal amount of practicality -- Rudolf I, Ferdinand I, Maria Theresa. And finally there was the group that has so often seemed characteristic of the whole line, the defenders of tradition, the old order, the conservatives and reactionaries pure and simple -- Frederick III, Francis I, and Leopold.[24] If Leopold does not exactly fit that typology it may be that another typology will find him a close analogue to Francis Joseph, as if by some strange coincidence the founder of the modern Habsburg Monarchy prefigured the man who would preside over its dissolution.[25] The value of such typologies is open to question, but they do direct attention to something that is not a matter of question, that is the indisputable fact that a Habsburg far more than other men, comes into the world with a very elaborate set of expectations and conditioned responses prepared for his official use.

The strongest force that operated on Leopold as a member of the House of Austria was his unquestioning acceptance of the fact that as Emperor he stood in a position of power above all the other monarchs of Europe. The Imperial crown had been a family possession so long that it took a positive effort to imagine it in any other hands but those of this doughty clan which had even in Leopold's time begun to treat it as a family heirloom. The Habsburg was not as other monarchs; Almighty God had called him and his successors to a position for which there were no equivalents in the temporal order. The wonder and awe produced by such a vocation might have encouraged arrogance and pride in most men, but for the elect it most frequently meant a heightened sense of humility. Charles V who in so many ways was the great exemplar for his heirs and successors in Spain and in Germany had found this vocation a burden beyond belief, and his abdication was a moving representation of what that superhuman responsibility had been for him in sorrow and in suffering. The emperors lived in the constant apprehension that their work would not find divine approval. Was it any wonder, then, that decisions were made only with the greatest soul-searching and that Habsburgs turned to the advice of their spiritual advisers long after other monarchs had abandoned such practices. There was something grandly archaic about this family view and, indeed, about the role the head of the house was required to play. Power had no attraction for those who continued to move within the limits of an age-old political theology where the king, the emperor rested under the heavy weight of taboo.[26]

This taboo found its expression in a regal idolatry that had few competitors. Thanks to the same Charles V the cult of the prince that had first taken hold in Burgundy had been adapted for Spanish use and had come to be known as the Spanish court ceremonial. Royal existence now became the province of a most complicated set of rules as every moment of the day and the very organization of the palace were transformed into instruments of the cult. Everything that might be spontaneous was banished from this unchanging system as unworthy of the ambience of a king, an emperor. For the modern observer of the court ceremonial the only reaction can be one of distaste if not of horror; how could one possibly preserve any freedom at all in such a stifling atmosphere?[27] For those who grew up within its limits there was a security and an inherent protective quality about it. Leopold would be found making use of it, too, as escape from his perennial quandary.

Austria had its *pietas*; it also had its *clementia*.[28] The first referred to the devotions to the Blessed Sacrament, the Immaculate Conception, the Holy Cross (this last particularly important in view of the belief that all earthly power rested ultimately on a *theologia crucis*). The second referred to the expectation that the Habsburg ruler would not indulge in unrestrained brutality or repressive measures, that moderation would be present in the midst of war and rebellion. Leopold's inherent benevolence found the *clementia* quite natural and acceptable, and though he had his notorious lapses from grace -- the Protestant pastors sent to the galleys would remain a blot on his memory -- he kept this family faith and instinctively shied away from anything that suggested tyranny. His notorious case of scruples helped to keep him on the right track.

The family tradition was not all private virtue writ large and translated into the realm of public affairs. There were avowedly political maxims as well, bits of Habsburg shrewdness that had been useful enough at one time to be passed on to succeeding generations. The Habsburg found it important and politically expedient not to reveal the true state of his feelings. Candor only made for difficulties; reserve and sweet dissimulation spared the man who practiced these arts the need to explain himself and to correct misapprehensions. Mystery became an emperor in any event, and the real secrets were destined for the confessor and for no one else. Leopold would find it enjoyable to have his version of the king's secret; he was not above hiding an integral part of a negotiation from the minister who had it in his charge. Dissimulation fitted in perfectly with another axiom: distrust one's ministers because they are likely to be the source of misinformation and mistaken policy. Leopold who happened to be suspicious of himself found it natural to be suspicious of others; only his evident liking for people overcame the hesitations he must have felt about their inborn ability to betray his interest and the good of his domain.[29]

Perhaps the most significant bit of Habsburg family political wisdom had to do with the manner in which the various parts of the Monarchy were to be treated. The Habsburgs more than any other European dynasty had found a home in a wide number of different locales. Much of this had been due to marriage and to sheer accident, but something of this power to adapt to local conditions might be traced to inspired common sense. Thus the Habsburgs, who were the most imperial of all the royal clans, also managed to have very deep roots in the provinces, and this encouraged them to believe that unity and diversity might go hand in hand. Charles VI was only giving expression to this tradition when he declared that he wished to "make a good beginning to the difficult task of governing both monarchies" (i.e., Spain and Austria) and that he was aware how little understanding there was in Vienna of the "method and system" existing in Spain.

> But this is now highly necessary because both monarchies must be considered equally... and there must be no difference between nations. All these lands should seek to be united under one ruler; every country will be governed best in accordance with its own privileges and customs; and it is therefore necessary for my service that I shall be sometimes in one country and sometimes in the other, and that some Spaniards go into my hereditary lands and some Germans come here, in order that they may understand the affairs of both as much as possible.[30]

Leopold's views can hardly have been different, though he did not have an opportunity to be quite so articulate on the importance of unified rule and official recognition of diversity in the form of customs and privileges. The scene was obviously set for one of the tensions discernible in his reign and one of the chief problems facing the members of the Deputation: how to reconcile the interests of the central authority with the interests of each land.

A man's character tells part of the story, and his family background an additional part, but something is left for the tender mercies of life itself. In 1697 Leopold had reached a point where his views and his policies had attained to a degree of rigidity that was only natural in a man rapidly approaching his sixtieth year. His lifetime had been full of contrasts between victory and defeat, and it was small wonder that the Emperor who had been forced to leave his capital so ignominiously in 1683 (he was to return shortly afterwards as something of a hero) would incline to the belief that all was changing and that victory or defeat were to be greeted with the same stoical calm. Looking back over a lifetime that had been full of uncertainty he might have regretted the fate, the Divine Providence that had decreed that he would not end his life the saintly ornament of an episcopal see or a noble abbatial lodge.

The Archduke Leopold Ignatius was born in 1640, the second son of Emperor Ferdinand III and his first wife, the Spanish Infanta Maria Anna, a daughter of King Philip III.[31] His older brother had been prepared for the crown it was assumed he would inherit while Leopold had been shunted off to preparations for an ecclesiastical career, a career much like that of his gifted uncle Archduke Leopold William, the Prince-Bishop of Passau. Though he was not destined for the greatest of all earthly offices and seemed quite content with his lot, he did rebel against the natural tendency of courtiers to devote all of their attention to his older brother. His mother's death when he was a boy had brought him face to face with a stepmother, and he was unfortunate to find in Eleanor Gonzaga a woman who would devote much of her attention and affection to the second son. His brother Ferdinand's death in 1654 changed all this, and Leopold was required now to abandon his learned pursuits and to prepare as best he could for his succession to many thrones. In common with most Habsburgs he had little practical preparation for his life's work; Habsburg emperors were notoriously reluctant to encourage their heirs to take an active part in affairs of state.

When he did succeed his father as a youth of eighteen he found that he would have to depend for a time on the advice, indeed the direction of older and more experienced men. This first period of his reign coincided with the influence of a chief minister on the making of policy. The gentle and unassuming Prince Portia, a former tutor of the young Emperor, held that post until his death in 1665, and then for nearly ten years the influence of Prince Lobkowitz was virtually unchallenged. Leopold had sworn at the death of Portia that he would be his own *"Primo Ministro"* in the future,[32] but it had been some years before he managed to carry out this threat. He knew how dangerous it was to depend on one man. The experience of his Spanish relatives with their *privados* could not be overlooked; it had generally been a disaster. Public opinion however primitive it might be expected that a ruler would take the reins of government in his own bands. Failure to do so was one of the most commonly heard complaints on the lips of those anxious to limit the royal authority.

The power of Lobkowitz presented Austria with a situation not unlike that which had obtained in France forty years before.[33] Austria might well follow the French example if Lobkowitz could manage to attain to the position which had been acquired by men like Richelieu and, more recently, by Mazarin. Lobkowitz represented more than a threat to the predominant influence of the monarch, he also envisaged an Austrian policy less enmeshed in religious and dynastic considerations. The doctrine of *raison d'état* appealed to him, and he could see applications of it that would turn Austria from its obsessive concern with Spain and the rivalry with France to a more productive role in Central Europe. Whatever else could be said for the man he clearly was thinking much ahead of his time and in ways that were not at all accessible to a man like Leopold I. Lobkowitz failed because his policy of rapprochement with France foundered on the rock of French aggression and the suspicion in Court circles that he was too pro-French for his own good and that of Austria. He failed, too, because he required the support of the Emperor, and no one, not even a Lobkowitz, could ever be sure of that. For such support was an abandonment of part of the onerous responsibility each Habsburg possessed, and such support was unlikely from a man who found himself constitutionally incapable of making up his mind and keeping to his resolutions. An opportunity to follow the French model was allowed to pass without much expression of regret. Leopold, though he was no Louis XIV, was no Louis XIII either, and as for men like Lobkowitz and the less impressive Auersperg, they did not even come within range of the two great cardinals.

But if absolutism in the manner of such men did not appear to take hold, there was still the chance that it might develop along the lines of bureaucratic reform and innovation, that is much in the manner of Colbert. Even before Lobkowitz had been sent away from court, a group of new men had begun to make their way up the official ladder. These were not magnates very much at their ease in this aristocratic Sion, but men of more humble background who had moved to Austria from the Habsburg possessions on the Rhine or from some small German state. They had received a university education and had managed to acquire those techniques, still largely legal, that were considered the most advanced style in public administration. Proximity to France had acquainted them with the latest French developments, and it would be no surprise at all when they began to display the same contempt for local customs that bad become characteristic of the French administrative system. As outsiders they failed to understand what was so sacred about ancient laws and privileges that were so often a facade for nobles who were anxious to flout Imperial decrees and patents. This was the second period in Leopold's reign, a time that has been called with much justice the period of "Absolutism Manqué (1671-1679)."[34]

Hungary could not fail to become the chief target of the innovators' zeal. It was the last important exception to the rule since Bohemia had been brought partially into line as a result of the battle of the White Mountain. Its leaders showed little desire to wait until their fate was sealed. They openly conspired against the Emperor and with

Louis XIV to a point where even Leopold decided that a new state of affairs would have to be established in Hungary if it was to remain a part of his possessions. A regime was installed in Hungary without any reference to existing laws or constitutions, and for a time it seemed that Hungary might be forced to adjust to the kind of treatment that was being meted out to it by men like Johann Paul Hocher, the Court Chancellor, and Christoph Abele, an official of the Treasury who was eventually to become its head. In the background the sweet reasoning of the Austrian cameralists could be heard, and though it is hard to believe that their contradictory and often enigmatic works had an impact on public life, they did at least point to the coming of a new political vision that was embodied in men like Hocher and Abele.[35]

The experiment in Hungary did not work for a number of reasons, not the least of them the fatal inability of its proponents to grasp the actual conditions in that portion of Hungary that was not under Turkish control or suzerainty. An additional reason and an important one could be found in the unwillingness of Leopold to break completely with the past and to turn over the direction of his government to men so clearly bent on innovation.[36] Absolutism in the style of his grandfather Ferdinand II had little power to trouble his conscience, but the more advanced and secular form propagated by a group of parvenus had to run head on into his preconceptions of his office and the constitution of his state.[37] The maxim about unity and diversity came quickly to mind. He had reacted strongly enough at the news of an outright conspiracy, but he would also react and quite as negatively to the plan for reordering Hungary on rational, that is unhistorical, lines.

By the time the original momentum of this absolutist phase had been lost -- Hocher died in 1683 and Abele retired from the office of President of the Treasury -- Leopold and his Austria found themselves compelled to take up a life and death struggle with the Turks. Austria had temporized for years on its eastern frontier, and a brief and not unsuccessful war with the Turks had been speedily concluded by the Treaty of Vasvár in 1662, so that Austria's hands would be freed for military activity in Western Europe. When the peace agreement which was to last for twenty years came up for renewal, Leopold had made every effort to continue the *status quo* in Austria's relations with Turkey. But the new Grand Vizir Kara Mustafa had other ideas, and thanks to the suggestions of the French Ambassador he was encouraged to direct his expansionist drive against Austria. It would be one of the many ironies of history that Louis XIV was thus responsible for initiating the third and most heroic phase of Leopold's reign, the undoubted rise of Austria as a Great Power.

Leopold had not sought heroism, and his role in the siege of Vienna was far from heroic. Yet by the end of that campaign Austria had gone over to the offensive and with the uncertain support of Poland, Venice, and the Holy See a great *Reconquista* began which was to win back much of Hungary from the Turks and open the way to Austrian expansion into the Balkans. Each campaign brought fresh victories, and Austrian generals (some of them German princes) appeared to be invincible for once. The old fears of imminent disaster and the reluctance to wager everything on the outcome of one battle or campaign disappeared, and even the classical rules of warfare which had been practiced as they had been preached by Raimund Montecuccoli were replaced by a military spirit that enabled men to take risks and to secure decisive victories. In that new spirit Charles of Lorraine, Max Emanuel of Bavaria, and the great Eugene of Savoy flourished. They were not alone. From all of Europe a stream of enthusiasts came to Vienna to try their luck, to vary a diet of aristocratic ennui, to find honor, riches, and death on the desolate frontier.

In the place of Hocher and Abele a new set of advisers appeared as Leopold turned to other sources of inspiration. The two key men were Count Theodor Althet Stratmann, who came originally from Cleves and had worked his way up in the Imperial service, and Count Franz Ulrich Kinsky, a gifted and difficult member of an old Bohemian noble family.[38] The two were soon in competition, and though Leopold reportedly loved Stratmann and only admired Kinsky he bad no intention of allowing one of the pair to emerge victorious from the contest. Even when Stratmann died in 1693, Kinsky still was kept waiting for the final goal of all his striving -- the post of Lord High Steward

(*Obersthofmeister*) which carried with it the honor of being the Emperor's chief adviser and the primacy of place in that most aristocratic Court. Leopold would dissapoint Kinsky on that score, and that disappointment would play some role in Kinsky's partial retirement from politics in the course of 1698 and his death in 1699.

War had been forced on Leopold by the Turks, and in the course of 1688 it became increasingly clear that he would have to fight Louis XIV. William III of England and the States of Holland were anxious to involve Leopold in a common effort to contain France, a proposal which could only find warm support in Vienna even if it meant alliance with heretics against the Most Christian King. But he was still at war with the Turks. To be sure, a Turkish peace delegation was at the moment in Vienna and an accommodation might be made despite the Turkish realization that the new war in the west strengthened their hand at the negotiating table. Leopold found himself caught between many contending forces and parties at his Court. *Realpolitik* in its primitive form virtually required his participation in the Grand Alliance; the real enthusiasm for the crusade against the Turks demanded that he fight until the Turks were ready to make substantial concessions to Austria and to Christendom.[39]

Leopold decided finally to take the enormous risk of fighting on both fronts, of containing France in the west, while his forces in Hungary continued to deliver punishing blows to the Turks. No one could imagine that he made this decision with ease. He was not the man for such easy decisions, nor was he unaware of the consequences of what he had decided to do. It meant nothing less than the ultimate degree of strain on his government and his subjects, and he took this step only in the confidence that God would not overlook his courage and his piety. As he explained to his friend and confidante Pater Marco d'Aviano, the great preacher who had whipped up so much enthusiasm for the war against the Turks:

> I shall bring all the power at my disposal to bear on these two redoubtable enemies. It will be extremely difficult, but it is not an outright impossibility, especially if the Princes of the Empire do their part vis-á-vis France. It certainly would be a thousand times better not to make peace with the Turks, as

that would halt any further advance of our holy faith in that part of the world. In any event, I shall not allow myself to enter into any agreement from which Christianity would not derive great benefit.[40]

His words were addressed to a very special audience, but there is no reason to believe that they were not an accurate statement of the Emperor's personal views. He knew that France had to be halted in its drive to expand, and he also knew that the crusade against the Turks had to be carried on until a great and permanent victory bad been assured. The indecisive Leopold had made the most important decision of his life and in so doing had laid the groundwork for the kind of financial confusion that required the good offices of the Deputation.

Such decisions came rarely to such a man, and even his readiness to fight on two fronts can be explained in terms of his basic reluctance to come down on one side or another in a number of crucial problems then facing his government and demanding more than temporary solutions.

The pursuit of the Spanish inheritance was one such problem.[41] It took priority over all other official concerns, and there can be no doubt that it was the largest single continuous undertaking of Leopold's reign. First by marriage, then by diplomacy, and finally by war, he did his best to ensure that the possessions of the Spanish branch of the *Casa d'Austria* would revert eventually to the German line. Yet even he had to realize that such an eventuality was remote indeed, that Europe would hardly allow the Habsburgs to recreate the predominant position they had acquired in the time of Charles V. Leopold had to take schemes for partition into account, and there was even reason to believe that what he hoped to derive from this policy was the possession of Lombardy and Naples. The will to world-monarchy was there, but political wisdom indicated that some kind of compromise would eventually have to be made.

Germany continued to be the source of anxiety and ambiguity.[42] The secular trend pointed to the withdrawal of Austria from German affairs. The conclusion of the Thirty Years War pointed in that direction; Austria had failed to make good its attempt to put the German house in order. Ferdinand III's disillusionment bad passed quite naturally to his son. But Leopold wavered and temporized here. He remembered that he was the Emperor, he responded to pressure from German princes and relatives, he even did what he could to preserve the western frontiers of the Holy Roman Empire without much success. A split was developing in the Austrian official mind between concerns that were purely German and purely Austrian, and Leopold's method of handling that problem was to make no firm commitment to either Empire or to his Danubian *Hausmacht*, the hereditary lands of reconquered Hungary.

Hungary now raised another problem which had not been of much importance before 1683, and that was the extent to which the Habsburgs should shift the burden of their political interest to the east, to Eastern Europe.[43] The basis of the family's power had always been in Western Europe, though the regional interests of Austria as such had been growing with the passage of time. Now a new perspective was developing that suggested that the path of greatness moved in an easterly direction. It was far too early to think in terms of an Austrian mission in the east, though the germ of such an idea could be found in the enthusiasm for the crusade against the Turks. But the balance between east and west which would become more critical for Austria in the course of its modern history had already appeared as a set of alternatives and options to be taken into consideration. In deciding to fight on two fronts Leopold had testified to his desire to keep these alternatives very much in mind.

An unheroic man with a profound incapacity for decision-making had been forced by the pressure of events to make at least one great decision and to take an important part in the heroic period of Austrian expansion to the east. Leopold looked out of place in all of this, and there is some reason to believe that he felt out of place. The old securities had disappeared, the timid policies that satisfied no one. In their place there had come wild oscillations between victory and defeat, between the possibility of greater power for Austria and its dissolution into fragments. In the midst of constant warfare that society required a postponement of the major issues that faced it. There was so little time and energy to think about finances, about the relations with the lands belonging to the House of Austria, about the inner constitution of one of the more exotic states of Europe.

Leopold, though he was not a heroic figure, fitted naturally in with that desire for a postponement of the great decisions. A policy of balancing alternatives came naturally to him and perhaps made him the kind of monarch that Austria required at that critical moment. His achievement when compared with Louis XIV would seem more impressive and even more permanent precisely because he had not been interested in going beyond the self-imposed limits, which had been developed in the course of his reign. He had chosen to react to events rather than to intervene in their formation, and the judgment of history, though it has so often been an unfavorable one still has to reckon with results, results that added something to the lustre of his name. And when his personal style of government and his program of sustained ambivalence is examined within the framework of his new administrative plaything, the Deputation, Leopold does not fail to gain something in political stature and personal charm.

Notes

1.   Alexander Navrokordatos to Count Kinsky, Pottendorf, March 23, 1689, *Documente privitóre la Istoria Romanilor*, culese de Eudoxiu de Hurmuzaki (Bucharest, 1885), V/1 (1650-1699), 242.

2.   M. der Ferdinandy, "Die Rolle des Königs: Die theatralische Bedeutung des spanischen Hofzeremoniells," *Der Monat* (XIX), #224 (May 1967), 148.

3. For Gualdo Priorato's difficulties in treating Leopold I from the standpoint of *virtú*, cf. Peter Moraw, "Kaiser und Geschichtschreiber um 1700," *Die Welt als Geschichte* (XXII), #3-4 (1962), 194-195, 199-200.

4. J. Fiedler, *Die Relationen der Botschafter Venedigs über Deutschland und Österreich im siebzehnten Jahrhundert* (Fontes Reruin Austriacarum, Abt. II, Bd. XXVII), Bd. II (K. Leopold I.) (Vienna, 1867); Arneth has a useful collection of Venetian contributions to a *Charakteristik* of Leopold in his *Prinz Eugen von Savoyen* (Vienna, 1864), I, 464-465.

5. G. Guillot, "Leopold I et sa Cour (1681-1684), D'apres la Correspondance et les Papiers personnels du Marquis de Sèbeville, Envoyé français a la Court de Vienne," *Revue des Questions Historiques* (LXXXI) (1907), 415-417; George Stepney's "short account" of the Court of Vienna has been published in the collection of *Prior Papers* found in the *Bath MSS*. (Historical Manuscripts Collection), III, 8-14.

6. Cf. Srbik's discussion of tbese memoirs, usually of French provenience, in *Wien und Versailles: 1692-1697: Zur Geschichte von Strassburg, Elsass und Lothringen* (Munich, 1944), 25-26.

7. Various versions of this picture of Leopold I are to be found in the following: A. von Arneth, *op. cit.*, 189-197; A. Gaedeke, *Die Politik Österreichs in der Spanischen Erbfolgefrage* (Leipzig, 1877), Bd. II, 58-61, for a generally unfavorable picture; Srbik, *op. cit.*, 25-27; "alles in allem, Kaiser Leopold I. war kein schlechter Herrscher, erst recht kein schlechter Mensch, ein grosser Staatsmann aber war er gewiss nicht, defür fehlte ihm, wie man nit Recht gesagt hat, die nachhaltige Kraft der wahren Herrschrnatur.", M. Braubach, *Prinz Eugen von Savoyen: Eine Biographie* (Munich, 1963), I, 100; for a very detailed and nuanced appraisal, cf. Thomas M. Barker, *Double Eagle and Crescent: Vienna's Second Turkish Siege and Its Historical Setting* (Albany, N.Y., 1967), 5-11.

8. Srbik, *op. cit.*, 25.

9.

10. P. Moraw, "Kaiser und Geschichtschreiber urn 1700 (II)," *Die Welt als Geschichte* (XXIII), #2 (1963), 105.

11. Stepney, *loc. cit.*, III, 9.

12. Guillot, *loc. cit.*, 416.

13. I have been struck by the way in which Leopold I fits the category of "Les Sentimentaux", a characterological type discussed at length by René Le Senne, *Traité de Caractérologie* (Paris, 1957), 209-291. Without entering into the question of the scientific validity of the work of the French school of characterology it does provide a basis, I think, for a unified treatment of Leopold's rather diverse character traits.

14. A. von Arneth, *op. cit.*, I, 190-191.

15. "Ama la musica...", Contarini's report, *ibid.*, I, 464; for complaints about the amount of money spent on the 'Musici', cf. M. Koch, "Beiträge zur neueren Geschichte aus unbenützten Handschriften," *Denkschriften der Kaiserlichen Akademie der Wissenschaften* (Vienna, 1850), Abt. II, 153. In 1670 43,702 (gulden) was spent on the musicians and only 36,420 on the *Reichshofrath*.

16. Contarii's report, A. von Arneth, *op. cit.*, I, 464.

17. This aspect of Leopold may not have received the attention it deserves. It fits in quite neatly with his dependence on the 'miracle of the House of Austra', cf. for the amount he spent on gambling, A. Wolf, "Die Hofkammer unter Kaiser Leopold I," *Sitzungsberichte der Phil. -Hist. Classe der Kais. Akademie der Wissenschaften* (XI), #1 (1853), 465 (Leopold lost 5,457 gulden in 1671), Roger Caillois, *Man Play, and Games* (Glencoe, Ill., 1961) discussion of games of chance is very important in this context, cf. especially pp. 145-160.

18. Gy. Szekfü, Magyar Törtenet (Budapest, 1935), IV, 180.

19. For an interesting discussion of his religiosity, cf. Barker, *op. cit.*, 9.

20. *Pietas Austriaca* finds an understanding commentator in Adam Wandruszka, *The House of Habsburg* tr. Cathleen and Hans Epstein (Garden City, N.Y., 1964), 128-130.

21. Rene Le Senne speaks of "résignation présomptive" in connection with 'Les Sentimentaux': "enfin *religieuse* quand nous prononcons: Que la volonté de Dieu soit faite/' en alléguant notre ignorance pour suggérer que cet événement qui nous semble mauvais doit manifester, sans que nous puissions savoir comment, la bonté divine.", *op. cit.*, 246.

22. Leopold's talent for making and keeping friends was to have a great impact on his conduct of government. The influence of his friends, his cronies, will become evident as the story of the Deputation unrolls.

23. A. Wandruszka, *op. cit.*, 131-137.

24. *Ibid.*, 8.

25. Heinrich Hitter von Srbik once compared Leopold I and Francis Joseph, but I have been unable to discover where he made this remark.

26. M. de Ferdinandy, *loc. cit.* for the most suggestive discussion I have seen of the deeper significance of the Spanish court ceremonial.
27. "In Wirklichkeit stand dem historischen Philipp II. nichts ferner,
als "frei und einzig" sein zu wollen. Ganz im Gegenteil in exemplar ischer Allgemeingültigkeit wollte er vor Volk, Dynastie, Hof und Kirche dastehen.", *ibid.*, 46.

28. A. Wandruszka, *op. cit.*, 130; T. M. Barker, *op. cit.*, 9.

29. "*Dissimular*, the dissembling of one's feelings, which Charles so
insistently recommended to his son, was cultivated by Philip to such a degree that he hid them not only from his contemporaries but also from posterity; for a long time Philip was thought to have been altogether incapable of emotion -- he had not just hidden his feelings but had never had any.", A. Wandruszka, *op. cit.*, 144. This picture of Philip II may be a key to the fairly common notion among his contemporaries of Leopold's lack of feeling, his stoicism. For one example of Leopold's treatment as a *stoicus*, G. Stepney to Vernon, Vienna, Sept. 8/18, 1693, S. P. F., 80, #17, 352.

30. J. W. Stoyne, "Emperor Charles VI: The Early Years of the Reign," *Transactions of the Royal Historical Society*, V Series, XII, 74.

31. In the absence of a modern biography of Leopold, I have relied heavily on Oswald Redlich's detailed treatment in *his Österreichs Grossmachtbildung in der Zeit Kaiser Leopolds I.* (Huber-Redlich, Geschichte Österreichs, VI), passim.

32. "... bleibe Ich Herr und kann em ander nicht vantiren, dass alles von ihm dependire; so kann ich es besser verantworten, dann alles ich mir selbst attribuiren muss.", Leopold to Potting, Feb. 18, 1665, quoted in A. F. Pribram, *Franz Paul Freiherr von Lisola und die Politik seiner Zeit* (Leipzig, 18914), 268.

33. Henry F. Schwarz has a most useful and perceptive account of Lobkowitz and his significance *in The Imperial Privy Council in the Seventeenth Century* (Harvard Historical Studies, LIII) (Cambridge, Mass., 1943), 151ff.

34. T. M. Barker, *op. cit.*, 28-36.
35. There is unfortunately no exhaustive modern treatment of Hocher and Abele. A Venetian reaction to Hocher at the height of his influence is to be found in Michieli's report which is excerpted by Arneth, *op. cit.* I, 466.

36. Szekfü, for all his sensitivity to the excesses of the "Wiener
Absolutisten", has no hesitancy is saying: "Leopold war kein überzeugter Anhänger der

modernen Ideen, wie sie ein Ludwig XIV. verkörperte. Die Machtstellung seines Hauses beruhte auf einer lebendigen Vielfältigkeit der Ständestaaten, von dieser Grudlage ist Leopold Zeit seines Lebens theoretisch nicht abgegangen. Er liess demnach seine Minister so lange nach ihren modernen Prinzipien frei schalten, als die Dinge nicht allzu schief gingen, dann griff er selbst ein und kam auf die früheren städischen Einrichtungen zurück.", J. Szekfü, *Der Staat Ungarn* (Stuttgart, 1918), 107.

37. Hans Sturmberger, *Kaiser Ferdinand II. und das Problem des Absolutismus* (Vienna, 1957).

38. B. Kuczynski, *Theodor Heinrich Althet von Stratmann* (Diss. Berlin 1934), 814.

39. Redlich, *op. cit.*, 417ff.

40. Quoted in Onno Klopp. *Das Jahr 1683 und der folgende grosze Türkenkrieg bis zum Frieden von Carlowitz* (Graz, 1882), 188.

41. A. Gaedeke, *op. cit.* remains the most detailed treatment of Leopold's involvement in Spanish affairs.

42. Henry Schwarz treats the tension between Imperial and Austrian emphases within the framework of the evolution of the Imperial Privy Council. "The inner conflict which arose out of this situation, which was, indeed,

Chapter Two
Verwirte Systema / Staff and Line

"... das gegenwertige verwirte systema..."
Count Philip Sinzendorf

The 'Leopoldinian system' owed much of its distinctive atmosphere to the personality and the political style of Emperor Leopold I, but it owed quite as much to the nature of the political and social context within which he moved. For if Leopold was the undoubted *sol* of the Austrian solar system, the summit of the social pyramid, and the final court of appeal in governmental matters he depended nonetheless on persons, parties, and institutions, on structures, both formal and informal, that had become synonymous with the Austrian Monarchy. These were the instrumentalities that executed his commands and helped him to overcome his hesitations; they were also able by their very nature to set definite limits on his freedom of action. He knew full well that he had to work within these limits, that he could never imagine that his actual power came even close to the family pretensions. If Leopold had been a more creative and decisive man he still would have had to reckon with these facts of political life, with the tendency of the Hungarians to rebel against an excess of centralization, with the reluctance of his loyal aristocracy to forget that their own political influence was often at stake. Indeed, it may well be that one of the most tangible achievements of this monarch with only a moderate gift for statesmanship was to honor the limits that he could in no wise change.

Much has been forgiven these Habsburgs out of a compassion for the difficulties they faced which seem now to have exceeded those that vexed Louis XIV or the Great Elector. The feeling has become widespread that the raw materials with which Leopold had to work were by their very nature less promising for the development of the modern state. But this may be to fall victim to a prejudice that assumes that political wisdom is the monopoly of any particular part of Europe, that we have to do here with a case of *ex occidente lux*. It may also be that we have a tendency to exaggerate the inadequacies of the 'Leopoldinian system', because we know less about its inner constitution and its workings than we do about developments in France or in England. Geography, history and chance had worked in wondrous ways in the Danubian region, and if Pufendorf was moved to describe the Holy Roman Empire as a *"monstrum"* he might have with equal reason used the same expression in regard to the Austrian Monarchy. Yet at the time, at the end of the seventeenth century, it had no monopoly on monstrosity, and, as for its fabled anarchroism, historical time had not yet made that point clear.

The structural part of the 'system' began curiously enough with a series of historico-political individualities, that is the lands comprising the Austrian Monarchy.[1] Legally that Monarchy was a loose union of nearly a score of kingdoms, principalities, duchies, counties, and marches, and their names -- Lower Austria, Upper Austria, Styria, Carinthia, Carniola, Tyrol, Breisgau, Bohemia, Moravia, Silesia, Hungary, Transylvania, Croatia, Slavonia, Dalmatia -- revealed enormous variety and a startling range of political and cultural possibilities. The Emperor acted as the link which bound these lands together in law, and on his succession each of the links in the chain had gone through the formality of recognizing him first and foremost as their sovereign lord, their king, prince, duke, count, etc. But this variety yielded something to regionalism after all. Austria, for example, usually figured as three 'provinces': 'Lower Austria' (the lands of Upper and Lower Austria), 'Inner Austria' (Styria, Carinthia, Cariola, etc.), and 'Upper Austria' (Tyrol and Further Austria in southern Germany).   This tripartite division had existed for some years after the death of Maximilian II (1576), and it was not until 1665 that Leopold managed to gather all these fragments into one and the same allegiance again. Each 'province' had its natural capital, and the tripartite division could be as easily discussed in terms of Vienna, Graz, and Innsbruck. The

Bohemian lands had two main divisions: the Kingdom of Bohemia proper and Moravia-Silesia. Hungary at this time remained in too fluid a state (it was in the process of being integrated into the Habsburg system) to speak with any certainty, though another tripartite divi sion appeared to make good administrative sense: the Kingdom of St. Stephen, Transylvania, which retained its special status even after its conquest by the Austrian army, and the triune kingdom of Croatia-Dalmatia-Slavonia, tied to Hungary by a real or personal union since the early middle ages.

This conglomerate state had a population of seven or eight millions, though that figure can hardly be more than an inspired guess in the absence of a census.[2] Still, the suggested total was imposing enough. It represented only half the number of the subjects of Louis XIV but more than held its own in comparison with most of the other states of Europe (with the exception, of course, of Russia). The area had been blessed with a wide range of natural resources and had particular strengths in arable land and in mineral deposits.[3] Any government anxious to look into the financial situation could assume that it was dealing with a rich and populous country, though the unfortunate consequences of the war with the Turks, a war that had in a very real sense been going on for a century and a half, left much of the territory recently won devastated and depopulated. Economic development lagged behind that of Western Europe for a variety of reasons, but one of the contributions of the Austrian cameralists had been to arouse a good deal of enthusiasm for the establishment of industry, the development of coimnerce, and the betterment of agriculture. The splendid vision of an Austrian at the head of the European class to be found in the work of Hörnigk, *Osterreich uber alles, alles nur will* (16814) seemed all too remote, but the materials were there for economic as well as geographical expansion; it was only a question if those who would be responsible for such improvements had the foresight and the energy to initiate new programs.[4]

The Monarchy that appeared so blessed in population and in natural resources looked hopeful, too, when it came to analyzing its administrative machinery. The Habsburgs had made an early start in the way of creating institutions for their Danubian dominions, and the councils and the *collegia* that had appeared in the sixteenth century were far in advance of most of Central and Eastern European practice. But this initial burst of creativity had not been sustained, and the Standing Orders of the sixteenth century made progressively less sense in the century that followed. To be sure, Leopold from time to time issued new instructions, but they proved on closer examination to be unimaginative copies of the original documents with a few small changes and emendations.[5] A central administration that had been advanced in the time of Ferdinand I, that barely held its own under Ferdinand II, had become obsolete and, what is more, chaotic during the reign of Leopold I. It survived on temporary solutions, occasional minor innovations that did not attack the root of the evil, and the wan hope that something would be done and soon just in time to prevent the whole machine from fragmenting into a thousand pieces.

The upper levels of this central administration looked harmless enough at first glance, and many a diplomat felt quite content to list the councils that assisted the Emperor and to leave the analysis at that. The Emperor was surrounded by councils, but the very number of these entities were at the base of his difficulties and that of his system. The Imperial Aulic Council (*Reichshofrat*) now confined itself to matters relating to the Empire. The Privy Council had devoted itself to Austrian affairs before it had become too unmanageable and had been largely superseded by the Privy Conference, the major advisory council on the most important affairs of state.   Then came the central organs of government, the Court Chancellery, the Treasury, and the War Council. They could claim direct contact with the Emperor on important matters, and yet all too frequently their affairs were minutely discussed in the Privy Conference. No clearcut hierarchical order existed here, and the modern student of public administration would be troubled by the absence of a clear distinction between staff and line functions. The Privy Conference might have confined itself to its advisory role rather than going beyond that to something that often approached a ministry. And the three *collegia* (with the possible additions of the Bohemian Chancellery and the General War Commissariat) might have felt more secure as the key departments of the executive, as the "*officia instrumentalia*" they were theoretically believed to be.[6]

The absence of a strong directing hand, whether on the part of the Emperor or on the part of a chief minister, meant that these bodies often worked at cross-purposes. They were all tempted in the presence of this vacuum at the heart of the system to assert themselves beyond their own strength. The Privy Conference, as we have seen, had tried to make the lyric leap from an advisory council to a ministry and had failed.[7] The Austrian Court Chancellery had grown from a mere secretarial bureau of the old Privy Council to something like the chief political office with far ranging responsibilities in domestic, foreign, and judicial affairs.[8] Men like Hocher and Stratmann had made the most of its functions and their influence, but when they were gone a weaker man had presided over the long-awaited reaction to the Chancellery's 'imperialism'. The Treasury had been badly tempted, too. What office was a more natural place for the dissemination of the new ideas and techniques of government than that which had charge of financial affairs, the chosen dimension for increased governmental activity? [9] Under a man like Abele it had briefly shown promise of rising above its place in life, but in more recent years it had lost something of this momentum and was now content to suggest innovations without being very serious about it. Finally, the War Council might pride itself on being the one *Hofmittel* that could with one slight exception regard itself as the Austrian central institution par excellence -- its orders were issued in all three parts of the Monarchy. The Imperial army had to be by its very nature a potent force in the political and psychological unification of the Austrian Monarchy, but the process was fated to be a long one and the War Council of Leopold I found itself in the early stages of its unifying work.[10]

This general perspective on the central administration suffers from being just that. To understand the perplexities of those who were involved in its workings it is necessary to take a closer look at its component parts. The Privy Conference, for example, had already experienced the fate of most Habsburg advisory councils; it had grown from a small and effective group of four to thirteen.[11] Since it could no longer pride itself on being a small group of the most influential advisers of the Emperor it met now not as one group but as a series of groups, as various members were deputized to talk about the war, the Spanish succession, Turkish affairs, finances, dynastic plans. The membership in these deputations fluctuated to some extent according to the wishes of the Emperor and the availability and interest (this could not be assumed) of individual members of the Privy Conference. There was the additional complication that the presiding officer of the Privy Conference and of many of its deputations was the Lord High Steward (*Obersthofmeister*). This meant that the chief officer of the Court (*Hofstaat*), a man wose claim to eminence was often more social than political, could, if he wished to do so, play an important role in administrative affairs. Members of the Privy Conference who also held key positions in the *collegia* found that they had to reckon with the inexperience and interest of a man who knew little of their daily concerns. This fact alone was sufficient to indicate that older forms of government persisted in Vienna; the Emperor had not yet brought himself to make a clearcut distinction between the government and the Court. The result, so far as the Privy Conference was concerned, was a mixture of responsible officials and the Emperor's cronies that did not provide the general staff work that was so urgently needed.

The Court Chancellery had existed since 1620.[12] Much of its life had been spent in competing with older institutions. It had struggled with the Imperial Chancellery for a voice in the affairs of the Empire, and when repulsed on that hand had turned to the work of undermining the Bohemian and Hungarian Chancelleries. This appetite for responsibilities left it a much sated office with such a multiplicity of tasks that it would not be long before it was divided in two. Its range meant that it would often tread on the toes of the Treasury and War Council; it shared its dominion over foreign affairs with the latter. It was broken down, according to the custom of the time, into sections on a regional rather than functional basis.

The Bohemian and Hungarian Chancelleries were located in Vienna and were charged with maintaining communications between the central government and the two kingdoms.[13] The Grand Chancellor of

Bohemia played a role in politics that often came close to that of the Court Chancellor, though it might be argued that this depended not so much on his office as on his personal influence with the Emperor. In Bohemian affairs he was assisted by an official, usually another Bohemian magnate with hopes of promotion to the post of Grand Chancellor, who supervised the work of the Bohemian Chancellery from day to day. All in all, this institution had held up well under most adverse circumstances, and there seemed to be sufficient local spirit among the Bohemian magnates to ensure that it would not suffer a permanent eclipse. The Hungarians had not been quite so successful in holding the line against Vienna's tendency to centralize. Their Chancellery had a subaltern look, and their Chancellor, frequently an ecclesiastic, did not treat with the other chancellors as an equal. He and the members of the Hungarian administration at Bratislava could not escapte the suspicion that they were outsiders merely tolerated by a government that would have preferred to use Germans in the administration of Hungary. Theirs was no enviable lot, for they were torn between their loyalty to the dynasty and their loyalty to Hungary's demand for a privileged position in the Austrian Monarchy.

The Treasury followed the usual collegial pattern in its organization.[14] In practice this meant a council with far too many councillors, presided over by a President and a Vice President. Its authority extended only to Austria and Bohemia (the Hungarians had their own Treasury which was in practice subject to the decrees of the central Treasury); it did manage to maintain its authority over the Hungarian mines.[15] Its contacts with local treasuries often depended on the mediation of the Court Chancellery, and since many of the funds that were collected locally were paid into the local treasuries and disbursed from there the Treasury had no overall control of funds within its jurisdiction nor any very clear idea of just what sums were involved. The absence of a central fund only further complicated matters.

The procedure for obtaining a vote of the *contributio* from the lands illustrates some of the problems the Treasury faced.[16] The Chancellery informed it of the day on which one of the local Estates would meet to consider the annual postulate of the Vienna government. The Treasury then had to consult with the treasury of the land in question as to what the practice had been, how much had been voted, how much had been received. This sum was then increased by a fairly large percentage so as to make certain that if only a portion was voted it would still come close to the sum that was actually required. The Chancellery took care of the details of these negotiations, and the funds, when they had been voted and collected, rarely found their way to Vienna.

If this did not underline the weaknesses of the Treasury it is important to remember that for over twenty years it had been presided over by a man who had done everything possible to destroy its usefulness. Count Georg Sinzendorf had managed to delude the all too trusting Leopold for nearly a generation before the truth of his incompetence, extravagance, and peculation could no longer be overlooked. His removal in 1681 allowed the Treasury to hope for better leadership (a hope that was to be satisfied in part), but the consequences of such monstrous mismanagement could not be corrected in a few years.[17]

The War Council had had as little chance to avoid the pitfalls encountered by most of these official bodies.[18] It suffered from a surfeit of councillors and paperwork, and its reaction to the campaigns in the field showed little speed and flexibility. No matter how much the generals needed official orders, supplies, and pay for their troops the War Council moved with a heavy-handed solemnity that was increasingly out of place if not downright dangerous to the cause of the Emperor. Tensions between the bureaucrats in Vienna and the fighting men consumed large amounts of official time and energy, and when, as was sometimes the case, a general of proven competence on the battlefield was elevated to the post of President of the War Council he was literally amazed at the confusion that reigned at the center of the military establishment. In no office did the collegial procedure have so many unfortunate consequences; everything came under the careful scrutiny of the officials, and no attempt whatsoever was made to distinguish what was important from the trivial.

This system could be forgiven for the confusions that arose over questions of military pay and supply. A rough and ready distinction along the lines of military questions and financial questions had been made by official fiat, but in practice this meant constant friction between the War Council and the Treasury with the Chancellery enjoying the spectacle from the sidelines. This had led in 1650 to the creation of a new office that received the resounding title of the General War Commissariat Office (General-Kriegs-Commissariats-Amt) that soon managed to find a niche of sorts between the Treasury and the War Council.[19] In practice it was expected to work closely with the War Council and to receive its funds from the Treasury. At least that was the official expectation. The practice, as always, diverged strikingly from the ideal. Its table of organization presented less problems, because it had few officials and was not organized in a collegial fashion. A General War Commissar had his headquarters in Vienna, while lesser worthies were attached to the armies in the field, aid still lesser worthies took charge of districts. In Prussian hands a device of this kind became one of the major instrumentalities in favoring the growth of centralization, but the Austrians did not realize what could be made of officials who dealt in food and fodder and soldiers' salaries that were long overdo. Though this office had been recognized as a *Hofmittel* and would be nominally represented in the Deputation, the *Mittelsdeputation*, in practice it did not even compete with the other central offices. Even its highest position remained unfilled for a long time, and the whole operation was headed up by an *Administrator*. Creaky machinery this was, and no doubt of it, and it would be an exercise in unravelling the mysteries of the official mentality to observe the Emperor and his advisers attempting to make it a bit more manageable. But any reform -- no matter how tentative -- did not embrace just the formal structure of administration; it could not help but involve the less structured elements of the 'Leopoldinian system'. Chief among those that were influential at the Court of Vienna were the amorphous political parties, the Emperor's spiritual advisers, and the Habsburg nobility, both as a cultural influence and as the holder of a virtual monopoly of high government office.

Political parties existed at the Court in Leopold's time, and one can assume that he cultivated their growth much as he encouraged the rivalries among his ministers. They prevented him from being faced with a consensus that would reduce his personal power and devalue his awesome obligation to God. These parties had even multiplied in the course of his reign, thanks to the encouragement they received. They provided one of the chief pleasures of foreign diplomats bent on establishing themselves as canny observers of Austrian affairs. Coenraad van Heemskerck, a Dutch diplomat who could not resist such a temptation, reported on them at length in 1691, when he gave what information he had to the States-General.[20] He claimed to have isolated no less than seven *factien*, a triumph in itself, and what he had to say about them suggests that these parties survived without much change down to the end of Leopold's reign in 1705.

The first party on the list was the Neuburg party which consisted of individuals at Court who were attached to the interest of that German dynasty. The Neuburg House had provided Leopold with his third wife, and it had also given Charles II of Spain his second wife. In addition to those triumphs it could count on the incessant activity of the ruling head of the House, the Elector of the Palatinate Johann Wilhelm.

Next in line was the Spanish party, a party with a great and honorable tradition at the Viennese Court. In the days when the Kings of Spain had constantly intervened in Austrian affairs the Spanish party had been an adjunct of the Spanish Embassy. Though that influence had declined as rapidly as Spain itself, the tradition remained, and the Spanish Ambassador, in this case the gifted Marques de Borgomanero, did all he could to preserve what influence remained.

There were then three small parties clustered together, the parties of Lorraine, Baden, and Bavaria. They formed about the princes of those states, who had secured great honors and prestige as generals in the campaigns in Hungary. Each party could also count on dynastic ties as well in winning adherents to their admittedly tiny conventicles.

In the rear guard there was the Austrian party. The mere fact that it came so far down on the list suggested that a Dutch diplomat may have allowed its background to influence his political analysis. But the Austrian party may have disappointed him for other reasons. Certainly, it reflected a growing self-awareness in the Austrian lands; it reminded those who would listen that it was Austria after all that had to be the focus of official concern. But the tone had not yet become assertive, and it would have to resign itself to long years of silent struggle with the dynastic involvements and universalistic aspirations of an Austrian monarch who could not yet bring himself to recognize that fact.

The last party on the list bore the name of the ecclesiastical party, an *omnium gatherum* any good Calvinist might construct in deference to the influence of the clergy and the religious in so Catholic a society. Its membership may well have been restricted to the more influential, to those who cared for Habsburg consciences and who filled the major ecclesiastical positions in the Habsburg dominions. Monolithic though this party would appear to an outsider, it had diverse strains within it. It had to take the policy of the Roman Curia into account and, at the same time, take cognizance of the interests of the local Churches. The religious orders maintained no common front, and their political perspectives followed no single inspiration. That this was a party cannot be denied, but that the influence of ecelesiastics could be reduced to being just one of a number of competing cliques remains very questionable.

Still, the identification of these parties represented something of a triumph (Van Heemskerck was not always so perceptive), but it inmediately raised more fundamental questions about the nature of these parties and the kind of policies they supported. 'Party' in such a context, did not do justice to a group that was so ephemeral and indistinct, so much a matter of personal taste and so little a question of political doctrine. 'Clique' came closer to the truth, since it underlined the fairly restricted character of the membership and the relative absence of leading ideas. For much of Leopold's reign these cliques were nothing more or less than uneasily concerted attempts to direct his main attention in one direction or another. They competed for his favor in securing positions and in advancing those who were favorable to their cause, but the cause, when closely examined, meant that Neuburg,

Spain, Baden, Bavaria, Lorraine, Austria, the Catholic Church should now assume a special role in his policy. They acted out as best they could and without being at all aware of it the options that existed for the House of Austria at the end of the seventeenth century, and in doing that they testified to the Emperor's will to maintain an ambiguous position, to avoid concentrating on one option to the exclusion of all others.

The Neuburg party favored emphasis in Western Europe largely because it had the Palatinate to consider, an area that had already felt the full brunt of French expansionism. The Austrian entry into the Grand Alliance had its support as a party, and the heretical views of the new allies presented no insurmountable problem for the Neuburgers. Stratmann, who may well have been the leader of this group, had been able, as one English admirer put it, to "mix a little politics with his religion", and the ordinary party member would easily fall in behind.[21] The Emperor's minister and chief confidante might not have exactly relished such a compliment; he had suffered much from being considered a parvenu by the Austrian nobles because he came of a lowly Protestant background.

The Spanish party had similar interests at stake. It could appeal to a more imposing prospect -- the revival of world monarchy -- but it suffered from the fact that it had been so long a staple of Austrian politics that its visions no longer aroused much enthusiasm. They did not fail, however, to find a response from Leopold in whom the family traditions remained a decisive force.

The Austrian party represented the opposite pole in the political argument carried on at the Court of Vienna. It could not attack the interest in Western Europe straight on, but it could point to the sudden and most unexpected increase in the Danubian *Hausmacht*. The triumph of 1683 had been a jolt to Habsburg traditions and complacency, and the very success that had been experienced in Hungary and in the northern Balkans encouraged some ministers and courtiers to think in terms of local issues. The Austrian party concentrated much of its attention on the war against the Turks; it showed far less enthusiasm for any western alliance that would permit Austria to be used for the greater glory and wealth of the Maritime

Powers.

The ecclesiastical party could support a similar orientation without experiencing any qualms of priestly conscience. The prospect of the continued struggle between Catholic France and Catholic Austria aroused little enthusiasm. What did inspire them was the crusade against the Moslems, particularly when it showed such continued signs of success. This crusade stirred memories that were not yet in danger of falling into complete discard; Christians were being liberated once again, while all of Christendom no longer had to fear a Turkish frontal assault. The Papacy had played a central role in organizing the crusade. Papal diplomats had urged the Powers to combine, and Papal funds had enabled them to do so. The atmosphere was undeniably archaic by the standards of Western Europe, but the ecclesiastics appeared quite unconcerned so long as the war went forward with every prospect of a successful conclusion.

In between the two poles -- east and west -- were the little parties devoted to the generals. This ambivalence should cause no surprise. At one time they could sincerely support the continuation of the war in the east. After all, it gave their heroes a chance to win additional laurels. At another time they were reminded that the hero had his interests as the ruler of a small German state or, as in the case of Charles of Lorraine, as the exiled ruler of a state that had been occupied by the French. Their views were ambiguous; they were also heavy with the provincialism, the *Kirchturmpolitik,* of small states that could not operate independently and that required help from more powerful neighbors and friends if they were to survive. The usual rivalries operated here: the party of Baden could not abide the Neuburg party, though both were often allies of the Spanish party.[22] The adherents of the Elector of Bavaria had to allay Austrian suspicions about Wittelsbach interests in so far as they ran counter to Austrian interests. It was possible to say on occasion that Bavaria and Austria had common interests, but not even the most zealous of the Bavarian party could fail to see that Max Emmanuel inclined to go his own way and, if that would help, to ally himself with Louis XIV.

It seems unlikely that these were the only recognizable groups at a Court that appeared to specialize in the creation of cliques. This list had been drawn upon the assumption that the cliques had as their main concern the making of Austrian foreign policy. But this only raised the question as to the existence of cliques concerned with domestic issues. The Deputation in the course of its discussions would indicate that there were such groups and that they were tied not to foreign states and interests but to regional traditions within the Monarchy. They played a role that has not been sufficiently appreciated, and they would survive beneath the conformity of centralization and rationalization to become the precursors of the aristocratic federalism that was to play so crucial a role in the emergence of political nationalism in Austria.

Informal political alliances that were directed to foreign affairs would obviously be of little help in discussing as important a domestic issue as the raising of funds to support a vigorous foreign commitment. The spiritual advisers of the Emperor and members of the dynasty would presumably be able to give even less assistance, though their role in the 'Leopoldinian system' provided the occasion for a good deal of misunderstanding. Foreign observers, particularly if they came from a Protestant country, never failed to linger on the pervasive character of this activity:

> I am now in a Place where Ecclesiastical Power is extremely great, that no person (that is not of their opinions) can be look't upon with any common Civility or obtain any advancement, assistance or countenance, that is not a Transubstantiationist, and therefore you may suppose negotiations go slowly, and heavily, while their Priests are continually buzzing in their ears Passive Obedience to Mother Church which forbids all concourse and sincerity of dealing with Hereticks... [23]

Many of the points which Lord Paget, and English Envoy Extraordinary to the Court of Vienna, listed in his indictment were unquestionably true. Priests did have a preponderant influence that went far beyond the limits of their cure of souls. They not only gave their advice on matter which touched upon questions of concience, but they often intervened in purely technical questions, as when they served as messengers or as 'experts' on military affairs. They did have a good deal to do with the selection of officials and with their subsequent careers, and it was unlikely that a man who was not a Catholic and who decided to remain in that heretical state would find any important opening in the Austrian service.

But the true nature of their contribution can only be understood in relation to the Emperor's character. He was too intelligent to accept their views without criticism, and, as for 'Passive Obedience' to the Church, he had enough of the traditional Habsburg belief in his right of intervention in church affairs to save himself from becoming a pawn of the clergy.[24] But this was not to say that he had no use for the services of a small group of priests, Jesuits for the most part; they could perform services for him that no minister or bureaucrat could undertake.

For one thing, these Jesuits enabled him to accede to the demands of *raison d'état* with far less feelings of guilt. These keepers of the Imperial conscience had made it possible for him to enter into alliance with heretics, to recognize William III as lawful King of England in place of the Catholic James II, and to grant the dignity of the Electorate to Protestant Hannover.[25] This hardly fits the pattern which Paget described, and good Protestant that he was he might have been even more horrified with the 'Ecclesiastical Power' if he had realized that it was often used to bring the Emperor around to decisions that were urged on him for admittedly secular reasons.

The Jesuit confessors helped him to make decisions simply by reminding him that he had to act in a way consistent with his responsibility to God. His ministers could give him arguments pro and con, but they were too involved in the internal dialogue and too dependent on Leopold's favor to speak so bluntly about the need for action. But a priest, who spoke in his capacity as God's representative in the spiritual realm, could speak his mind and bring a subtle pressure to bear on the decision-making process.[26]

In regard to the careers that they advanced the Jesuits were often responsible for making a positive contribution to the government service, because they could advance those who had real promise. Considerations of family and *Stand* had less influence on them than it did on the Emperor and his ministers, and in a time of crisis it often devolved upon a father confessor to point to the man or men who would set things right. Eugene of Savoy owed much to the Jesuits, for it was Pater Bischoff who was largely responsible for his appointment as President of the War Council of 1703.[27]

These very real contributions to the well-being of the Austrian government have often been overlooked in the perhaps natural desire to resent an influence coming from an ecclesiastical source. Leopold and his government desperately needed informal sources of information, tips on likely people for the service, and an ideological perspective that admitted o some compromise with the world. Indeed, the worldliness, rather than the excessive religiosity of some of these men, was cause for adverse comment. More than most men in that milieu they were open to some of the rawer currents of thought in Western Europe; they were even more struck by the necessity of bringing Austrian political practice into line with these advances. It was no coincidence that the Jesuits were active in this process of secularization. They had always served an ideal of sanctity in the world, of a religious commitment that went hand in hand with the demands of great responsibilities to society. At its best this was a form of Christian humanism that could not fail to be attractive in its best representatives; at its worst this ideal degenerated into the most mechanical adaptation to secular utilitarianism.[28] The moments when this impulse to bring the Christian life into the palace and the counting house broke down were numerous, and they provided ammunition for the kind of frontal attack mounted by Pascal in his *Provincial Letters*. Yet in their way these priests felt that they were serving God and His Church. Their presence was required by the structure of that society and the personality of the Emperor; they carried out a number of crucial tasks and, in so doing, the were responsible to some degree for nudging Austria, even the 'bigoted' Austria of Leopold I, along the road to modernity.

The political parties contributed to the liveliness of the discussion of Austria's putative role in European affairs, and the Jesuits made their contribution, if often by indirection, to the secularization of the political process. The Habsburg aristocracy, the paladins that jealously guarded the Imperial throne, also played an important role in the system, though it is not quite so easy to describe. It grew out of the fact that this *Stand* dominated the central administration and the Estates, that it served the Emperor and provided the last defence of local rights and liberties. It gave society its characteristically aristocratic air and did much to embellish the Austrian towns and countryside with the best of Baroque art and architecture. Everywhere one turned in Leopold' s Austria the presence and the power of this social order were manifest.

The increasing monopoly of high public office which they had achieved during his reign did much to determine the manner in which his government operated.[29] For these aristocrats did not leave their code of conduct at the office door; they experienced no discomfort at all in making their official employment but another facet of a life which was not governed according to the ideals of rationality and efficiency. A high percentage of aristocrats in the governmental machinery did more than anything else to prevent it from coming to grips with important domestic issues.

For one thing the aristocrat who was also an influential member of the government had relatively little time to devote to public affairs, since he followed a daily schedule that allowed him little time for work. The day of even one of the more diligent of these aristocratic officials was instructive.[30] He did not rise before eight in the morning or arrive at his office before nine Official meetings occupied his time until noon, when his work ceased in effect for the day. After a visit to the Hofburg or to a friend it was time for dinner at two o'clock. This meal lasted sometimes for two or three hours and was often taken at the townhouse of a friend or at a *Sommerpalais* of the family outside the city walls. After dinner he took a nap or played cards. The evening was devoted to society, and it was usually midnight before he retired. That *horaium* applied to a day on which the *collegia* met or dispatches had to be prepared. On feast days, which were disconcertingly numerous, and many other 'work days' even less attention was shown to official business. In that atmosphere a man who kept to his office, did not drink or play cards, and managed to get through large amounts of paperwork was regarded as something of an oddity. Though it might also be noted that such oddities often managed to work themselves into responsible positions because they were so useful to the Emperor.

When the aristocrat was hard at work, his approach to matters that came to his official attention tended to be 'cavalier', a phrase that was common in the period to describe a fairly typical lack of professional concern.[31] A light and glancing blow (often.endowed with much intelligence) was the best that could be managed; routine and long periods of continuous work had to be left to those whose social position had not prevented them from being *gründlich*. This does not mean that the aristocrats could not produce an occasional bureaucrat of real talent and application to business, and it does not mean that their talents were not useful to the government. They made excellent generals and diplomats if only because valor and representative functions were their chosen state of life. Intelligence, when they possessed it to any degree, found its expression in the contemplation of the larger issues, particularly in the realm of foreign affairs. Details bored them, and often they had the good sense to acquire the services of subordinates who did much of the legwork and who, for that very reason, often acquired an acknowledged position in governmental circles.

Financial affairs did not inspire much enthusiasm in the mind of an aristocrat, though a few -- Count Quintin Jörger and Count Thomas Gundacker Starhemberg -- acquired a reputation for their knowledge and their probity in administering the Imperial finances. Jörger's suggestions as to the personal characteristics of a good President of the Treasury throw an interesting light on the need to combine social prejudice and some thought of technical competence. He believed that a likely prospect should be honest, informed, without too many relatives, stable and independent of the high officials of the Court. It was expected that he would come of a distinguished family, because he would be required, particularly during time of war, to treat with kings, electors, and ambassadors. A prelate would not fit this bill, because the Abbots of Kremsmünster and Lilienfeld, who had held the post in recent memory, had not exactly distinguished themselves. Finally, this paragon of virtue should be well-bred, not given to gambling or banquetting, straightforward in his dealings, and unembarrassed by debts.[32]

All these forces (and others as well) went into the sublime mixture that constituted the 'Leopoldiian system'.   It had its evident strengths: the reliance on tradition and on traditional elites, and the ability to make modifications without appearing to do so. But it suffered from an impressive nunher of weaknesses. Some of these might be found in any political system: the *lenteurs*, the reliance on administration rather than on political creativity, the overwhelming need for better-trained personnel. Other weaknesses reflected the stage that Austria had reached in its understanding of its internal constitution. The balance between the center and the peripheries still leaned dangerously in favor of the lands and their Estates. The central administration was top-heavy; the councils and the *collegia* had developed far beyond the capacity of subordinate or, better, insubordinate bodies to keep up with them. And the personal style of Leopold had its obvious impact on slowing down the evolution in the direction of a viable ministry, of departments of government worthy of the name, and the appearance of the political scene of a figure other than the Emperor who would take chief responsibility for the operation of the government. Society and not Leopold determined that most of the available people for governmental responsibility would be aristocrats, and their culture ensured that foreign affairs would receive more attention than domestic affairs and that the bureaucratic process would obey the aristocratic code rathern than its own inspirations.

Yet even a system that promised so little in the way of any concerted effort to talk about the cost of war and where and how the money should be raised to foot the bill had to face that issue sooner or later. In this instance it was, of course, later, but some decision could not be delayed forever. And when the official discussion began with ever so much hesitation and uncertainty it took place within the frame of the much maligned Privy Conference. If that body could not come up with an answer to these questions it could at least set a chain of events in motion that would lead after further hesitations and delays to the creation of of the *Deputatio des Status Publico-oeconomico-militaris*.

Notes

1. Luschin von Ebergreuth, *Grundriss der österreichishcen Reichsgeschichte* (Bamberg, 1899), 210-292, may well be the most concise and useful introduction to the political and social structure of the Austrian Monarchy; cf. the remarks of Otto Hintze, "Der österreichishce und der preussische Beamtenstaat im 17. und 18. Jahrhundert: Eine vergleichende Bertrachtung," *Historische Zeitschrift*, LXXXVI (1901), 401m.

2. For one set of census figures, cf. *Feldzüge des Prinzen Eugen von Savoyen* (Vienna, 1876), Ser. I. Bd. I, 86, 91.

3. "Cosi servito dal Consiglio de' suoi Ministri siede Leopoldo sul Trono, et estende il Scetro sopra Corso de' Paesi ampio nel giro, abbondante ne' Popoli, felice per molti doni della natura, e specialmente per I Tesori raccolti nelle Miniere di tutt'i Metalli, ch'aprirebbero copiosa la sorgente delle rechezze, s'anco in esse volesse più applicarsi l'industria à moltiplicarne I profitti.", Carlo Ruzzini in his Final Relation on his Embassy at Vienna and the Congress of Carlowitz, 1699, *Die Relationen der Botschafter Venedigs über Deutschland und Österreich im siebzehnten Jahrhundert*, ed. J. Fiedler (Fontes rerum austriacarum, Abt. II, XXVII), Bd. II (K. Leopold I.), 397.

4. Philipp Wilhelm von Hörnigk, *Österreich über alles, wenn es nur will*, ed. G. Otruba, (Vienna, 1964), 51-52 especially.

5. As, for example, the *Hofkammerordnung* of 1681, Fellner-Kretschmayr, *Die Österreichische Zentralverwaltung* (Veröffentlichungen der Komission für neuere Geschichte Osterreiches, V) Abt. I., Bd. I, 89-90.

6 G. Turba, *Reichsgraf Seilern aus Ladenburg am Neckar 1646-1715*

als kurpfalzischer und österreichischer Staatsmann (Heidelberg, 1923), quotes Count Jörger, "Es ist aber wissendt, dass die Hoffcantzley nur ein officium instrumentale (Amt als Vollzugswerkzeug) ist, welches mit dem *universo* nichts zu thun hatt.", 197.

7. H. F. Schwarz, *The Imperial Privy Council in the Seventeenth Century* (Harvard Historical Studies, LIII) (Cambridge, Mass., 1943), 187.

8. Otto Hintze did much to develop the notion that the Court Chancellery played a role of the utmost importance in the development of the Austrian central administration. Cf. *loc. cit.*, 416-418, where he also makes the interesting point that it would be of interest to follow this development by studying the individual court chancellors.

9. J. Szekü, *Der Staat Ungarn* (Stuttgart, 1918), 108.

10. "Der Hofffkriegsrat wurde das festeste Bindemittel der habsburgischen Länder.", Fellner-Kretschmayr, *op. cit.*, Abt. I, Bd. I, 241.

11. The best discussion of the Privy Conference is to be found in
Henry Schwarz, *op. cit.*, 166-190; cf. also Fellner-Kretschmayr, *op. cit.*, Abt. I. Bd. I,
53-57.

12. Gustav Turba presents a most interesting description of the state of the Austrian
Court Chancellery just at this time, *op. cit.*, 187-202.

13. Fellner-Kretschmayr has a chapter on the Bohemian Court Chancellery, *op. cit.*,
Abt. I, Bd. I, 174-217; on the Hungarian Chancellery, cf. Gy. Ember, *Az újkori magyar
közigazgatás törtente: Mohácstol a török kiuzéséig* (Magyar Országos Levéltá
Kiadványai, III), 113-119.

14. Adam Wolf, "Die Hofkammer unter Kaiser Leopold I," *Sitzungsberichte der
Philosophisch-historischen Classe der Kais. Akademie der Wissenschaften*, XI (1853),
#1, 440484.

15. Gy. Ember, *op. cit.*, 119-147. The dependence of the Hungarian
Treasury on the Court Treasury is nowhere more explicitly and characteristically stated
than by Leopold I himself in answer to a complaint of the Treasury about the Hungarian
Treasury: The Hungarian Treasury is subordinate to the (Court) Treasury; one should
make that clear to the Hungarian Treasury without any harsh expressions.", *Hoffinanz,
Ungann*, CCCLXXXVIII (März-Juni 1698), 43-50.

16. A. Wolf, *loc. cit.*, 455-456.

17. *Ibid.*, 475-481.

18. Feldzüge, Ser. I, Bd. I, 190-194; O. Regele, *Der österreichische Hofkriegsrat 1556-
1848* (Mitteilungen des österreichischen Staatsarchivs, Ergänzungs-Band I) (Vienna,
1949), 19-21.

19. Feldzüge, Ser. I, Bd. I, 194-195.

20. Van Heemskerck believed that the absence of a chief minister was one of the major
causes for the development of the parties, cf. C. van
Heemskerck to the Pensionary, Vienna, Nov. 13, 1691, *Weensche
Gezantschapsberichten van 1670 tot 1720*, ed. G. van Antal, J. C. H. de
Pater (Rijks Geschiedkundige Publicatien, 67) (The Hague, 1929), 494ff.

21. G. Stepney, *Bath MSS.*, III, 9.

22. Van Heemskerck's report, *loc. cit.*, 498.

23. Lord Paget to Sir (?), Vienna, May 3, 1690, *Add. MSS.* (British
Museum) 8880, fol. 14.

24. The role of the Habsburgs in the Catholic Reformation has often
obscured the fact that they were confirmed supporters of a tradition of
Staatskirchentum, cf. Luschin von Ebengreuth, op. cit., 252-253; J. Wodka, *Kirche in
Österreich: Wegweiser durch ihre Geschichte* (Vienna, 1959), 287-290.
25. As Srbik suggests the picture presented by the activities of the politically active
Fathers of the Society of Jesus at the Court of Vienna differs somewhat from the
conventional picture, cf. his *Wien und Versailles 1692-1697: Zur Geschichte von
Strassburg, Elsass und Lothringen* (Munich, 1944), 41-44. For their advice on crucial
decisions, *ibid.*, 44.

26. The Venetian Ambassador Morosini in his Final Relation of 1674
expressed the opinion that the Jesuits had encouraged Leopold' s indecisiveness by
reminding him how necessary it was to act with a clear conscience; they did this,
according to Worosini, from "more secret and worldlier motives," *Relationen der
Botschafter Venedigs*, 144. But a survey of their activities suggests a more active and
positive role in the decision-making process.

27. For Eugene's tie with Bischoff and the role it played in the dismissal of the old guard
and Eugene's appointment as President of the War Council, cf. M. Braubach, *Prinz
Eugen von Savoyen* (Vienna, 1963), 354-367 passim.

28. R. Spaemann, *Reflexion und Spontaneität: Studien über Fenelon*
(Stuttgart, 1963), 136n.

29. In the absence of a detailed study of this problem, i.e., the manner and the
importance of aristocrats in the Habsburg service the lists of office holders in an
appendix at the end of Fellner-Kretschmayr, *op. cit.*, Abt. I, Bd. I, 273-288, are
suggestive.

30. Based on the admittedly prejudiced but perceptive "Relazione
della Corte di Vienna del conte San Martino di Baldissero (1713)," *Relazioni
Ambasciatori Sabaudi, Genovesi e Veneti* (1693-1713), ed. C. Morondi (Bologna,
1935), I, 114.

31. "Weniger 'kavaliermässig' und mit mehr "Gründlichkeit' musste
gerade in der österreichischen Hofkanzlei gearbeitet werden: Worte, die der
kurpfälzische Kanzler 'Wiser,' auch bürgerlicher Abkunft, gegenüber dem Grafen Kinsky,
Seilern zuliebe, 1697 schon desergen freimütig äussern dürfte, weil Kinsky ein genauer
Herr war, also nicht 'kavaliermässig' arbeitet.", Turba, *op. cit.*, 193.

32. Jörger's introduction to his 'Gutachten über die Finanzen, April 14,
1679" is used as a source in J. Graf Mailath, *Geschichte des österreichischen kaiserstaates*
(Hamburg, 1848), IV, 379-386, for the traits to be looked for in a President of the
Treasury, cf. page 381.

Chapter Three
Instruction / Guidelines

The Deputation looked brand-new when it emerged after an uncertain period of gestation in the late fall of 1697. Nothing quite like it had existed before. There had been a plethora of committees, permanent and impermanent, but never a coordinating committee that comprised the central organs of the Viennese goverment. The *"Ordnung und Instruction"* that set down the rules under which it was to operate indicated that the Deputation was to be an integral part of the "newly established and regulated politico-economico-military establishment." [1] The table of organization, the well-defined area of responsibility, the list of do's and don't's all testified to the fact that a splendid young instrument of governmental deliberation and execution had come upon the scene.

Yet its novelty, as is so often the case, could not but be more apparent than real. It was not that anyone could point to the existence of a proto-Deputation, to an attempt at a coordinating committee that had been tried and had failed. But there had been meetings within the framework of the Privy Conference that resembled those of the Deputation in more than one respect. The same officials had been involved; the same general problem had been discussed. Even the forms of thought and expression were the same. So it must be said that when Emperor Leopold I and Count Kinsky, who must share the honor of having been the creator of the Deputation, decided to innovate by creating a new committee they were not forced to depend too heavily on their imagination. What was more likely was that they had tried a number of things to alleviate the financial crisis and had finally come to the point where only an entirely new committee could be of assistance.

A year before the Deputation appeared, small subcommittees of the Privy Conference were already engaged in a serious discussion of the extent to which Hungary would be expected to contribute to the military budget.[2] In planning for the *contributio* for 1697 the Privy Conference had set its sights high and had informed the Hungarians that they would have to pay four million gulden rather than the two million gulden they had paid in recent years. This lyric leap suggested that the responsible officials who could entertain such an idea had not taken leave of their senses but rather were in such a state of desperation that they were forced to look for an easy victim. Hungary seemed a likely prospect. Large portions of the country had been freed for some time from Turkish rule, and presumably it had recovered sufficiently to be able to pay more in the way of taxes. Then, too, the Hungarians were thought to be so grateful for their liberation that they would strain to do their utmost for the Emperor. Besides, Austria and Bohemia had borne the brunt of the war for so long a time that they could not be expected to provide additional revenues now. No, all the signs pointed to Hungary, and an optimism that was part unalloyed hope and part desperation took hold in the minds of these Austrian officials. The only question that remained was the degree of resistance this order would arouse in Hungary.

The chief ministers and their aides, the *referendarii*, the career bureaucrats who assisted them in their deliberations, sat down one day to ponder the Hungarian response to the demand for four million gulden.[3] The Palatine of Hungary, Prince Paul Esterházy, had doubtless consulted with the members of the royal administration in Bratislava and with the *Palatine Concursus*, the committee that represented the Hungarian Diet in tax negotiations when the Diet was not in session. The Palatine's response was conveyed to the members of the subcommittee in his absence, since he was not a member of the Privy Conference. On occasion he and, his aides would be summoned to a meeting as an exception to the rule; on this occasion his remarks on the subject of the tax were reported to the committee by Hofkammerrat von Palm.

For any minister who might have nourished the hope that 'gold' would be discovered in Hungary the report from Esterházy ended all illusions. The Hungarians did not prevaricate; they said flatly and finally that they would not even listen to the figure of four million.[4] They had been paying two million gulden and had hoped that this sum would be reduced rather than doubled as now seemed to be the idea. The negative response was as solemn as the Palatine could make it, and, as if to ensure that the ministers would not misunderstand the Hungarian position, a whole list of grievances (*gravamina*) had been tacked on to the initial refusal to go along with a doubling of the war-tax.

The list consisted of twenty-one articles, and after the manner of all such lists it contained complaints that were by then all too familiar to the Austrians. But for those who listened closely and with even a minimal effort to understand the list could constitute a telling condemnation of Habsburg policy in Hungary. The Hungarians objected to the way their own privileges were ignored and their own officials overruled. They did not have sufficient part in the work of the commission on the *Neoacquistica*, lands that had been conquered from the Turks but that had not been returned to Hungarian administration and ownership. They lamented the sad condition of the royal Hungarian cities that had been deprived of their ancient liberties. The separate identities of the Hungarian and Transylvanian Chancelleries struck them as a mistaken step; what was needed was their unification (a step in the direction of the return of Transylvania to full participation in the life of the Kingdom of St. Stephen). They also criticized the fact that there were too many troops in Hungary and far too many of them became a burden on the Hungarians when they went into winter quarters ("Half of the amy should spend the winter outside of Hungary."). And border questions under dispute between Hungary and Poland and, this was an interesting sidelight on the Hungarian mentality, between Hungary and the other parts of the Monarchy should be settled soon and with the assistance of the Hungarian Chancellor.

The show of resistance in this official answer to the Austrian prayer forced the ministers to look to other as yet untapped sources of revenue. They could not afford to be too discriminating or finicky in view of the disastrous financial situation. If Hungary had failed them they would consider a project to introduce a fairly complicated system of excise taxes. Such a tax on the consumption of goods already existed, though in a most incomplete and disorganized way, so the excise tax could not be considered a real novelty from the point of view of Austrian practice. But the ministers who discussed it believed that something as all-embracing and as rich in revenues as they were considering could indeed qualify as new and untried. They would certainly think of it in such terms. The project before them did not go into details, and it would be necessary to secure more information, particularly on the numbers of inhabitants of the lands, and more detail on just how the plan would operate.

Treasury expressed the belief that the excise tax project had great promise.[5] Excise taxes had been introduced in other countries and had been successful. They worked so well because everyone had to eat and to drink, and this universal requirement ensured that everyone in this society would be bound to contribute his portion of the tax. Yet for all their enthusiasm and their apparent grasp of what was involved in such a plan, the financial experts did not convey much in the way of conviction; they were grasping for straws quite evidently and unable to hide the fact from the more perceptive of the ministers. Kinsky, for one, could not be carried off on this new wave of enthusiasm. He was prepared to admit that one could not be too careful in locating new sources of revenue, but he was hesitant in this instance, because it seemed that a project that had been conceived in haste and without being worked out in detail might have the frightening consequence of undermining the existing tax system.[6] No one could deny that it was faulty as it stood, but it did produce a certain amount of revenue every year, an achievement that might be well beyond the possibility of the excise tax system. Kinsky always saw the difficulties in any decisive action, and his personal taste ran to the balancing of alternatives and their consequences, but when it came to the excise tax he was on even stronger ground than usual in framing objections.

In addition to the knotty question of whether or not such a plan was practicable there was also the question of how the governnent should negotiate such a tax with the lands. Inevitably this would mean discussions in Vienna with deputies from all parts of the Monarchy, and such discussions might well produce no action and, in addition, the same kind of negative reaction that had been encountered on the part of Hungary, when the four million gulden had been mentioned. The spectre of a General Diet of the Austrian and Bohemian Lands never failed to trouble the Emperor's ministers, and they handled the question of the deputies from the lands who were to discuss the excise tax in a most gingerly fashion. At one moment the latest hostility between the Lord High Steward Prince Ferdinand Dietrichstein and Kinsky came suddenly to the surface. Dietrichstein gave his opinion that the deputies should be chosen by the central administration, the chancelleries in this case, without going through the intermediary agency of the local governments. Kinsky took such a dim view of this opinion that he expressed the wish that the prince would confine himself to remarks that were to the point. Dietrichstein obviously resented Kinsky's behavior and replied that he was doing just that.[7] This exchange was to have its companion piece in another instance of Kinsky's loss of control and display of impatience. Dietrichstein reported on another occasion that there was a man in Silesia who had come up with a plan to tax cattle. This project claimed that the tax would net twelve million
gulden which fit in admirably well with the sum that was now most often quoted as the optimum for the military *fundus*. "The Lord Kinsky laughed."[8] It was as simple and as natural a reaction as that. Though it could only serve to exacerbate the relations between the man who was chief minister in all but the name and the man who was chief minister in name (Lord High Steward) and in little else, that laugh must have come from the heart of a minister who had heard so many similar crackbrained projects proposed as panaceas.

Another minister who was much in evidence at these meetings took even less care to spare his audience. This was Leopold Cardinal Kollonich, Primate of Hungary and former president of the Court Treasury and the Hungarian Treasury. He was the acknowledged expert on Hungarian affairs in the inner circle of Austrian ministers, and his expertise was amplified by the fact that he felt the full weight of his responsibility to the Hungarians. As he expressed it, he was to Hungary in his capacity as primate what the Pope was for all of Christendom. And now as these discussions on the tax project followed the usual pattern of Viennese *lenteurs* he could not hide his truly primatial impatience. The Habsburg Monarchy was threatened to the extent that its very existence had come into question, and this naturally meant that the future of Christendom itself was a matter of doubt. He found it difficult to understand that the ministers went about their business as usual; they were evading their responsibilities to the Emperor if they did not give him the advice that was needed in a time of crisis. As if to counter the unspoken feeling that he was making himself unpopular by speaking such homely truths he declared himself quite ready to go into retirement in Rome, where he would receive a pension from the Pope and another and even larger one from the King of Spain.[9] Kollonich had powerful emotions and a gift for sounding the alarm. He had had a long and more than usually heroic career as a Knight of Malta and as an Austrian and Hungarian prelate. But he was decidedly less impressive when it came to the constructive suggestions that he felt should be made. His wealth of experience and the very force of his emotions played him strange tricks. One minute he could believe that ten million gulden (and not the optimum twelve million) would probably be sufficient; it had certainly been quite enough when he had been in charge of the Treasury. At another moment he gave his solemn assurances that the Hungarians were in fact able to contribute four million gulden; indeed they could do better than that figure without excessive strain.[10]

Towards the end of these discussions on the excise tax Leopold I had a brief opportunity to give his views. The moment came at the end of a meeting of the entire Privy Conference, when it seemed that a final decision would be made on whether or not to proceed with the carrying out of the plan. The Emperor agreed that the usual sources of revenue were now insufficient and drew the conclusion that one had to think seriously then about introducing an excise tax. It seemed to him that responsible people with some experience should be summoned to Vienna to discuss the details of the program.   The whole business needed a lot of work and developing, and in this line he expected that all the offices would do their utmost to cooperate and to make a useful contribution. The political, the military, the financial offices should do what they could to carry the project forward, an anticipation surely of the exact nature of the future Deputation. He underlined the need for participation and cooperation by expressing the belief that the Emperor 'could not manage the whole thing by himself'; he would need the assistance of his central administration. Words failed him after that, and all he could say in conclusion was that the work was now to begin in earnest.[11]

But even this show of decisiveness did not ensure that the project would be carried into operation. At yet another meeting, which Leopold did not attend, the summoning of the deputies was discussed once again, and the general enthusiasm for the project had clearly declined. Kinsky had become even more alert to the dangers it presumably contained by stating that it would be difficult to carry out because the "lands differ in their constitution, in their manner of livelihood and paying taxes." Both generally and specifically the project raised more questions than it answered, and Kinsky's reluctance to commit himself and the Conference to the excise tax may then have spelled its demise as a practical means of raising revenue.

Whatever the outcome (and the protocol of the Privy Conference gives no hint of what happened after this) the Conference had a very different problem to discuss in the summer of 1697. The excise tax appeared to be forgotten, and the hope now rested on a general reorganization of the system of paying and supplying the troops. The Austrian army had acquired the unattractive reputation of being the most burdensome for the unlucky individuals among whom it took up its quarters, especially during the winter months. The cost of the upkeep of the army often ran far beyond the tidy sins discussed in the meetings of the War Council and the Treasury. The practice of allowing the regiments to live off the country -- often the Emperor's dominions -- gave way in the course of the seventeenth century to the issuing of a series of ordinances that regulated the payment and provisioning of the army. Such a Supply Ordinance (*Verpflegs-Ordonnanz*) came up for discussion in the Privy Conference in 1697, because previous efforts to reduce the burden imposed on local authorities and populations by the presence in their midst of the troops had broken down. Hungary, for example, had reportedly been required to spend as much as four or five million gulden during 1696, and this in addition to the sum it had to pay in war-tax. The new Supply Ordinance hoped to remove a large member of inequities by regulating the exact pay and food ration for each military rank irrespective of where a military detachment might be stationed. The discussion of the details of such a project required great learning and experience in matters of military finance. For most of the ministers it was an occasion to display their expertise in so esoteric a field and also to reveal how prone they were to seek for salvation from bankruptcy by pitching upon such a device.[12]

The discussion in the Privy Conference can be followed in great detail. Never had the members had too much to say on any single question, and never had they been reported at such length. Prince Dietrichstein favored the ordinance, though his support could not be described as unqualified, he looked for more economy throughout the administration to produce the desired results. But he managed to remain sanguine. So far he could see help was in sight if only one did not lose time. Kinsky came next in line, and he, too, pointed to the confusions in military and financial affairs. The Treasury said that it was at the end of its resources and that the future of twelve million gulden was the outer limit of what could be expected from the lands. The local governments continued to report the excesses of the military, and when they had recourse to the War Council, they received no satisfaction at all unless impudence could be called a satisfaction. Still, this measure represented for Kinsky the best that could be managed under the circumstances. If anyone had a better idea as to how the money should be spent on the military, if he knew more about such matters, he must now prove that this was the case.[14] It was not exactly optimism that moved Kinsky at the prospect of putting this Supply Ordinance into effect, but he knew full well that any move of this kind was bound to create difficulties.

The other ministers followed in order, and most of their *vota* revealed a similar awareness of the difficulties, combined with a most moderate hope that the new system would work. But two men made no secret of the fact that they did not favor innovation: Heinrich Mansfeld, Prince of Fondi, the Lord Marshall of the Court, and Count Ernst Rüdiger Starhemberg, the President of the War Council. Mansfeld, who was an old friend of the Emperor's, had a variety of reasons for his opposition. The *fundus* of twelve million gulden was excessive in the first place; the lands could not be expected to produce so large a sum. He then went on to criticize a number of detailed provisions of the ordinance which related to the equipping and paying of the troops. But the theme that ran through everything he said could easily be disentangled from the mass of details: the old system (a cynic would have said the lack of it) bad worked well enough and everyone had grown accustomed to it.[15] Starhemberg began his statement by roundly declaring that he had nothing but praise for what Mansfeld had said. He resented criticism of his official bailiwick and mentioned that Kinsky had been misinformed when he had reported that the War Council had been allowing important matters, i.e., the protests of the lands, to be completely overlooked. The doughty old warrior felt that he and the military establishment had come under attack at the very time that it had produced a string of great victories for the dynasty. This intervention in its affairs, mounted by a group of men who were specialists in political and in financial affairs, struck him as a monstrous piece of ingratitude.[16]

The upshot of this conference was that the figure of twelve million became the norm for the war-tax and the Supply Ordinance, doubtless with further revisions, became the law of the land, a dignity it was to preserve until another such ordinance was issued in 1699. These meetings had touched on a number of themes that were intimately tied to war, taxation and reform, and it had become increasingly clear that the Privy Conference, as a whole or in small groups, had done all that could be expected of it to assist the monarch whose plaintive cry might continue to be: "I can't do it all by myself." His experience of the inability of the Conference to came to grips with the major issues and, at the same time, to smooth out difficulties that came up in the actual administration of the Monarchy compelled him now to act with an unaccustomed energy and decision.

He could not have chosen a more propitious moment to act. For that point had been reached in a literally endless war that gave him and his government sufficient confidence in the final victory to permit them to engage in some stocktaking at home. Statesmen and political leaders experience a wonderful sense of elation then and indulge themselves in the illusion that they are making a fresh start. With the grim business of managing to do little more than survive safely behind them, they can and do begin to plan on measures that had long been postponed under the pressures of war.

However 'stoical' Leopold may have been by nature or design he must have participated to some degree in the pleasing events of September 1697. During the month the Grand Alliance made a great advance in negotiating a treaty of peace with France at the Dutch town of Rijswijk, and the sane month witnessed Eugene of Savoy's first great victory in his defeat of the Turks at Zenta. The two events, the peace negotiations and the battle won, produced a lightening of spirits in Austrian official circles. To be sure, the Austrian diplomats would not be pleased with what they managed to secure for Austria at the conference table, and the Turks continued to mahe martial noises even while they slowly accommodated themselves to the dreary fact that they had been decisively beaten and must begin to negotiate peace. As if to cast further doubt on the wave of euphoria, Ferenc Tokaji put himself at the head of an uprising in Hungary that looked to the leadership of Prince Ferenc II Rákóczi, who was to lead an even greater uprising in 1703. But the brief interval between wars and the encouragement of a kind proferred by the uprising did much to create the atmosphere in which the Deputation could evolve as the newest and latest device for handling a perennial problem.

Leopold' s interest in completing the work of organizing the new military "*status*" had been expressed in his support of the Supply Ordinance and his interest in a number of related orders and decrees. It may well have been that Kinsky deserved the honor of inventing the

Deputation, though it would seem clear that Leopold took the leadership in making sure that this idea becsme a reality. On November 24, 1697, he issued a decree which created the Deputation and gave his reasons for calling it into being.[17] Shortly thereafter he took note of the fact that Kinsky had written a *"Regulamentum"* for the new body and had begun to complain of all the work it had involved in addition to his duties as the Grand Chancellor of Bohemia. The Emperor said that he realized how busy Kinsky had been but that he thought it absolutely essential that he act as its *praeses* -- "that you not only attend the... Deputation but that you direct its work as *praeses*." In view of this additional burden Leopold suggested that much of the routine work of the Bohemian Chancellery could be turned over to the Vice Chancellor. It was his intention to entrust the new committee entirely to Kinsky, to allow him to do what he wanted with it, and to listen to none of the complaints against him that might result from this new position of trust.[18]

The *"Ordnung und Instruction"* of Dec. 10, 1697 put the finishing touches on the work of preparation.[19] It may well have been a revised form of the *"Regulamentum"* on which Kinsky had worked so hard; it was long enough and detailed enough as a state paper to warrant a certain amount of discreet complaint on the part of the author, particularly when there was reason to believe that Kinsky did not share the Emperor's enthusiasm for their latest piece of administrative handiwork. These instructions went into so much detail and took into account so many possible situations that it is difficult to imagine anyone else but Kinsky as its author with a few changes by the Emperor to bring it into line with his customary official style.

At the very outset the declaration was made that the Deputation would consist of "our court chancelleries, Treasury, War Council, and General War Commissariat", a statement that looked innocent enough as it stood though it gave no satisfactory picture of the actual membership. It then went on to lay down the guidelines for its work: the questions that it was to discuss, the procedures it was to follow in deliberating and in executing its decisions, the whole range of topics that were included within its area of influence.

Before these were set down in detail there was a reminder of the reasons for establishing the Deputation. It had been created in the hope that there would be better discipline in the army, that the lands would not suffer so much from their would-be defenders, and that their contributions would be paid in a more dependable way, that the means for prosecuting the war would not be insufficient. All these signal improvements in the condition of the military establishment would surely owe much to a body in which matters relating to its financial and political aspects were discussed and where the usual excuses of imperfect communications and placing the blame on some other office would have the ground cut out from under them.

But any innovation constituted a threat to the existing system, and the Instructions vent on to emphasize the point that the various chancelleries and agencies of government retained full authority on matters which were directly under their authority or which could be handled without recourse to a coordinating committee. But in any matter that had by its very nature to be treated in common the Deputation had the right to deliberate and presumably to take final action. Examples of matters that came within the jurisdiction of the Deputation were negotiations with the lands in connection with military matters, questions of the good order of the military establishment, and attempts by one party or another to increase the funds at the disposal of the military machine.

Those general headings may have been felt to be still too general, so a more specific list of matters that should be referred to the Deputation followed. Complaints arising from military excesses and disorders along the line of march, inequalities in the distribution of the war-tax or in the quartering of troops, the recruiting and equipping of soldiers, the arrangements that were to be made for the passage of a military detachment from one part of the Monarchy to another, sudden crises that arose which required extraordinary services and funds, the computation of the number of troops for a campaign and how much money would be needed to maintain them, the obstacles encountered by such a plan, lack of bread and fodder, deficiencies in equipment, the support and maintenance of fortifications, armories, naval detachments, the lack of supplies or when they were too expensive, the *contributio* and additional means of military support, the discovery of additional means of support over and above the usual quota so as not to be prejudicial to the lands, and, finally, when anything had to be decided *collegialiter*. A long run-on sentence as this was, it managed to cover a good deal of ground and to convey as little else could the Baroque style of the instructions. Any office that received a complaint or a report of any such developments was required to bring this to the Deputation's notice at the very next meeting. Every care was taken that a remedy might be quickly found, and this in a generalized sense most fittingly described the *raison d'être* of the Deputation. The matters that had been included in the breathless canvass of matters calling upon the Deputation for its attention had overlooked the heart of the problem, the "nervus aller geschäfte," money.[20] There then followed a long section devoted to the *fundus* of twelve million gulden and how it was to be divided among the Monarchy's taxpayers. This division was obviously made with an eye on the old calculus of the Treasury: Upper Austria paid twice as much as Lower Austria, while Inner Austria equalled their total contribution; Bohemia paid twice as much as all of Austria put together with a breakdown of four-ninths for the Kingdom of Bohemia, two-ninths for Moravia, and three-ninths for Silesia.[21] The pattern was followed to the letter for Austria: 810,185 gulden for Lower Austria, 405,093 for Upper Austria, and 1,215,278 for Inner Austria. The figures for Bohemia indicated that Bohemia paid exactly one-half instead of four-ninths; Moravia was down to one-sixth; Silesia held its accustomed place at three-ninths. But when the document moved on to Hungary and Transylvania all the crabbed computations disappeared in the relentless desire to discover hidden treasure. Hungary was listed for four million gulden, and Transylvania was expected to contribute one million. Of the grand total (and surely the men of the Deputation would have reason to realize just how grandiose it was) Bohemia and Austria were required to pay sixty percent; Hungary and Transylvania, a much weaker combination, as much as forty percent. The scheme made it painfully evident that Bohemia-Moravia-Silesia had been contributing and was expected to continue contributing the largest bloc of the war-tax, though Hungary was now seen to be a close competitor at least in theory. As if to make the impression even more compelling each land found its total broken down into monthly contributions with an additional sum that was to be paid after arrangements had been made with the Treasury.

The *fundus* predated the existence of the Deputation, and there was apparently little that could be done but to accept the twelve million gulden as a point of departure for the difficult negotiations with the lands. But once that figure had been accepted in theory, the Deputation was to pay particular attention to the breakdown of the tax at the local level, the so-called "*Repartition*" so as to make sure that it was done according to proportion and fairness. This was to prevent the local authorities from shifting the burden of the tax from those who could pay to the weak and unpropertied. Secondly, every effort was to be made to encourage the local officials to collect the taxes according to the *Repartition*, and at this level, too, no partiality or connivance with reluctant taxpayers was to be permitted. Thirdly, the *gouverni*, the heads of the governments of the various lands, were to submit weekly reports of the money that had been collected and forwarded to the General War Chest (*Generalkriegskassa*) or to its local branches. If the taxes were in arrears these men were required to file a report on the circumstances, so that a remedy could be quickly and effectively devised to ensure the uninterrupted flow of gulden.

The chancelleries had an important stake in overseeing this operation, for they were to watch for these signs of slackness and inefficiency at the local level. Once they became aware of any difficulties they were to take steps to secure the entire sum that had been assigned to an individual or a land that could not keep up its payments. And if this did not work the Emperor declared that he stood ready to throw the full weight of his authority behind the admonitions of the chancelleries to the guilty parties.

The Treasury, too, had special responsibilities that related to the collection of the *contributio*. Since it would be some time before the full sum could be realized (and there were nine million gulden in current debts that had to be serviced along the way) it was to do its best to ensure the proper management of the funds once they reached the war chest or its local branches. The Treasury decided then how they were to be distributed (the General War Commissariat looked after the actual distribution.) Once again, the Instructions asserted that it was not intended to make any substantial modification of the usual procedures in collecting and dispersing the funds. So as to assuage any displays of temper at the War Council notice was also given that its wishes in regard to the material aspect of war were not to be overlooked. To make this all the more likely, weekly meetings between representatives of the Treasury and the War Council were to be scheduled. And in the course of this tour of interests that had to be taken into consideration reference was also made to the poor taxpayers. Their confidence was to be sustained by giving them real assurance that everything they contributed to the military establishment went directly into the military budget. It was expected that this would only serve to increase the taxpayers' enthusiasm for the Emperor's service and have a positive effect on the size of their payments.

In the transitional period that led to the firm establishment of this system, a number of temporary measures were envisaged that might cause difficulties and confusions. It would be necessary to sustain the government's credit and to engage in additional borrowing. The Treasury would have to divert funds from the Cameralétat (virtually all other sources of income) to the military budget in the expectation of the eventual arrival of the twelve million gulden. Suggestions were made as to how the debt might be looked at more closely with an eye to maintaining credit and easing the interest payments. There could be no doubt that the maintenance of credit depended on the satisfaction of a number of leading creditors. These individuals were to be paid in full and on time. Less important creditors faced the possibility of being asked to accept a longer term of repayment and a smaller percentage of interest. There was even a third group of creditors who might now expect to receive the bad news that payments on their loans would have to be postponed to better times.

So that the Deputation might be enabled to follow the whole range of financial operations already discussed in the Instructions it specified the creation of a new office in the Treasury, the office of War

Comptroller (*Kriegsconrtolor*). The man who was to assume this post was expected to be an initiate of the mysteries of double entry bookkeeping; this would permit him to keep a journal of every financial transaction that had to do with the *fundus*. To facilitate his work protocols of the meetings of the Treasury and the Deputation were to be placed at his disposal, so that he would miss none of the official directives that originated in these committees. This did not mean that "the old order should be disturbed"; everything else was to remain as it had been according to the ancient usage. But now, weak points in the system could be spotted immediately, thanks to the overall view of the War Comptroller; and once the Treasury had been informed, it could take the proper steps to set matters right.

The Instructions referred in passing to the Supply Ordinance, and then expressed the hope that the Deputation would devote some of its time to reflecting on the problem of inflation and the rise in prices that resulted from the pronounced enthusiasm for luxury throughout the Emperor's dominions. The Deputation had other odd jobs: it was to make proposals on the status and pay of officers not on active service and to discuss a proposal from the General War Commissariat concerning the appointment and salaries of certain classes of War commissars.

Its meetings were to take place on Monday and Thursday mornings; the *praeses* was to notify the members on the previous day that a meeting would be held. In the event that nothing had been proposed for discussion, a meeting might be cancelled. If one or more of the members found that they could not attend, it was their responsibility to see that a replacement was sent from the same chancellery or office.

It was time now for a peroration that would serve to bring together all the major points that had been covered and to provide a certain motivation for the onerous work ahead. No one was to be left in doubt as to the critical importance of the Deputation's work: it addressed itself to no less a good work than the security and welfare of the lands which God had entrusted to the care of the Emperor. This made it mandatory that each deputized councillor was to think of nothing but the common good and to work in complete harmony with his colleagues. With this cooperation ensured, a heart-warming state of affairs would soon result: the military establishment would find itself in good political and financial condition, the lands would contribute what they were expected to contribute, the soldiers would receive their pay on time, and not one of the interested parties -- the lands, the Treasury, the army -- would have any reason for complaint. This idyllic picture was then related to committee procedures. The Deputation, because it acted with one heart and one will, could make its decisions on the basis of a majority of the votes of the members. If the minority appeared to have unusual strength, however, the matter under discussion was to be referred to the Emperor, as was anything else that could be described as a matter of real importance. But the usual practice would allow the Deputation to decide what was to be done and then assume that the members (and the agencies they represented) involved in carrying out that decision would take responsibility for its execution. This led to the making of a somewhat academic distinction between the deliberative function of the Deputation, that is when it acted as a body, and the executive function that was located in those responsible for carrying out its wishes. The Emperor felt confident that in making such a distinction he would be better able to discover the source of the trouble in the event of a malfunction. What he found most reassuring, of course, was his belief that with his new committee hard at work it would be virtually impossible for officials and agencies of government to make excuses; they would no longer be able to say that they had received insufficient information or that they had not received it in time, and there would be less likelihood of shifting the blame to the other fellow.

The moment had come for the inevitable conclusion:

> Accordingly, we look to these our councillors in the Deputation for the very best and rely entirely on their prudence, loyalty, industry and zeal. With these qualities they will know how to supplement and put into practice those things which if they are not expressly mentioned in these Instructions are yet covered by them in a general way.

The Emperor's "unwavering will and opinion" had found expression in an exceedingly long and complicated document that was evidence of the care that had gone into the planning for the Deputation. Few Austrian official bodies could boast of so much imperial solicitude at the time of their parturition, and even fewer could point to an *Ordnung und Instruction* that was a minor masterpiece of the genre of administrative guidelines in its ability to combine a general perspective of the Deputation's activities with a lively awareness of the difficulties that would be encountered in practice.

If the document fell short in any way it might be said to sin against a unified impression; it had an obvious reluctance to be all of one piece. Even the most casual reader -- and what casual reader would be likely to attempt so involved an official text? -- had to be struck by the striking differences in tone, the sudden shifts of gear, the evident soundings of vastly different depths of thought and expression. This patent lack of homogeneity might be traced in part to the men who were most responsible for the character of the Instructions: the Emperor and Count Kinsky. By their very nature they did not incline to forthright and unambiguous statement; they had their own good reasons -- they were not the same -- for preferring mystery to absolute clarity. For the Emperor such an evasion provided a release from the tyranny of committing himself finally and irrevocably to any one line of action, while for Kinsky it grew out of a basic refusal to compress the complexity of any problem or situation into a formula that was pat or monochromatic. Still in this particular instance they had some excuse for refusing to be tied down too neatly: the Deputation that they envisaged was expected to operate on two different levels. The first was almost exclusively administrative in character with the emphasis on the improvement of administrative techniques. The second was at the highest level of domestic politics and concerned the nature of Hungary's relations with the rest of the Austrian Monarchy.

The first level, the administrative one, was developed with a good deal of specificity at the beginning of the Instructions. Here all the many instances of administrative confusion were described with unerring realism and ticketed as impediments to an effective *"oeconomi"* and *"policei"* of the military establishment. Without some such field expedient as the Deputation Austria might find itself incapable of responding to the challenges of continued war and international tension simply because its official machinery was on the verge of a complete breakdown. The Deputation had its beginning then in the search for a solution to problems of administration, and it proposed itself as a device, a commonsense device, for handling the literally innumerable cases of mismanagement, departmental rivalry, and bureaucratic willfulness. Many of these cases were unimportant in themselves, but in the mass they pointed to weaknesses of the system that were as chronic as they were laden with disastrous consequences.

The assignment to create some order at the highest levels of Austrian government should have been more than sufficient for one committee, but it also discovered that its fate was intimately connected with the knotty and perhaps insoluble question of Hungary. For in the very process of discussing the administrative role of the Deputation the Instructions turned with even greater force and conviction to the monetary heart of the matter which in this instance meant Hungary. A certain degree of official tact prevented the Emperor and Kinsky from making this plain; Hungary was mentioned only in passing, but it was clearly uppermost in their thoughts when the sum of four million gulden was mentioned (and an additional million from Transylvania) and when they laid down the rules for a just repartition of the tax. Hungary sinned most flagrantly against an equitable distribution of the tax, and the practices of circumventing even the original repartition were most inveterate there. The Hungarian noble clung to his refusal to be taxed with a violence that might shame his opposite number in Austria and Bohemia, and his rigidity in thinking about a whole range of political, constitutional, and social problems stood as the main obstacle in the way of Hungary's integration as a full-fledged and dues-paying member of the Austrian Monarchy.

The intent of this section was clear. Behind a facade of tax reform in pursuit of the chimerical twelve million gulden the Austrian government hoped to make more satisfactory arrangements for itself in Hungary. This was an old device of state-builders to begin with a distressing but apparently innocent appeal for funds and to use that as the opening wedge for a wide range of changes and reforms. Hungary had already taken a few hesitant steps down the road already traversed by Austria and Bohemia: it had recognized the hereditary claim to the Crown of St. Stephen of the House of Austria, and had abandoned its *jus resistendi*. But now even more was asked of it, and there was good reason to believe that the kind of repartition envisioned by the Instructions threatened the preservation of Hungary's traditional constitutional and social forms. All the while the Austrian official mind refused to admit that it was actually engaged in a reform that verged on revolution. When pressed it could only say that it was high time for Hungary, recently restored to Christendom and the House of Austria, to pay its own way. Any committee that had to devote itself to carrying through a program that doubled the *contributio* and demanded that the Hungarians abandon their obsolescent privileges might have wished for another and kindlier fate. The Deputation, finding itself saddled with the 'Hungarian question', could take small comfort from the fact that it had thus been handed the most critical problem of Austrian domestic politics with a commission to pursue a tough and unrelenting line.

Expected as it was to operate on such different levels of magnitude, the members of the Deputation might well have complained that these levels required markedly dissimilar talents. The administrative tangles called for a microscopic vision, for infinite patience, and for a continual will to produce face-saving compromises. Prolonged involvement in such trivia could only result in a complete inability to think in broad and creative terms. Yet this was exactly what they were expected to do in dealing at the political level with the Hungarians. Enormous intelligence, infinite energy, a perfect sense of timing, ruthlessness that could be combined with occasional acts of charity and compassion -- these were the qualities required of them by the Hungarian problem. The gap between the gifted administrator and the statesman widened here into an abyss, and if it was highly unlikely that one man could manage to excel in these two realms it was quite as unlikely that one small group of men would have any better luck.

Yet the major obstacle to a unified Impression was not individuals and their psychological makeup or the variety of assignments that had been given to the Deputation but the clear presence of two divergent mentalities in the official mind itself. Though men like Leopold and Kinsky were presumably quite unconscious of this state of affairs what they had written and approved constituted proof of a most suggestive kind for the view that they were men with split personalities when it came to *Weltanschauung*. At one moment they were comfortably ensconced in the traditional world of the aristocrat, in a patriarchal ideology that laid claim to being eternal. In another moment they revealed a different side, one that had much in common with the rationalistic categories of the bourgeoisie and the professional bureaucrat. These two mentalities existed side by side without apparent contradiction or competition in that happy period when the struggle for undivided mastery had not yet begun. Lines were not yet drawn with any precision or finality, and traditionalism retained a primacy of honor, though its patent inability to respond to the increasing demands placed on government required even the loyal Court of Vienna to cast about for more effective alternatives.

The very language in which the Instructions were written underlined the crisis of the old order. For the official language of the Court of Vienna had a splendidly archaic quality of its own that found few competitors in the domain of German speech. While other German Courts played with modish French phrases, the Austrians continued to brace their homely German with large infusions of Latin and occasionally borrowings from Italian and Spanish. The hegemony of Latin culture persisted in Vienna with an intensity that was no longer possible elsewhere, and this was a form of Latin culture that, if it had not lost its beauty, bad a diminished claim on the best minds of Europe. The result was that those who were called upon to frame a document like the Instructions did not have available to them a form of expression that could do justice to either their traditionalism or their tentatives in the direction of modernity. Their chosen form was cosmopolitan enough for a multinational political community, and it did provide something of a bridge to the Hungarians who persisted in their attachment to Latin as their official language. But it lacked precision, brevity, and dash, and when it approached an issue it did so with a maximum of indirection before strangling it to death with a welter of dependent clauses and repetitive phrases. The latter-day devotee of the Baroque might find this attractive and even impressive without fully grasping the confusions that this argot produced and the way in which it added only further complication to the presence of two sets of mental and emotional responses.

Traditionalism, as it found expression in these Instructions, had a necessarily limited vocabulary in German or in Latin. It lingered long and lovingly on the will to remain true to custom (*"nach dem alten gebrauch und herkommen"*) and gave notice that the old order, an order which was thought to be inimitable, should not be troubled in any way (*"die alte ordnung in nichts turbirt werden"*). Weaknesses in it that had become so manifest were thought to be imperfections rather than standing invitations to forthright change. Indeed, it was assumed that once the *"confusiones und verrungen"* had been removed the "true usage of the ancient custom" would emerge in its pristine purity.

The model upon which this mentality operated was that of the patriarchal family in which it was a simple matter to equate God, the Emperor, and the father. This family existed for the safety and security of its members, and it would be preserved by an obedience to custom and to its major expositor, the head of the house. Here the emphasis rested on cohesion, consensus, a unanimity of mind and heart (*"in guter harmoni und mit vereinigtem gemüth und herzen"*). Failure to respond to the deeper impulses of this established order would produce the inevitable return of a primeval chaos. In a political context this spectre was expressed in the ruination of the lands (*"die länder... zu grund gerichtet"*). Matter-of-factness which is so often a companion of the traditional view could under the rapidly changing circumstances verge on unconscious irony: there was a statement to the effect that the taxpayers, once they had full assurance that the money they were contributing went into the military treasury and to no other end, would "experience an increase of love and trust... and have a greater desire and motivation to contribute..."

How different was the other mentality that expressed itself here, that made no mystery of its belief that efficiency more than any other single factor should call the tune. "Good management" became an end in itself, and what was needed to achieve this blessed state was not loyalty or obedience but adequate knowledge (*"fundamentaler wissenschaft"*), hard work, and punctuality. The pointed interest in a steady flow of reliable information could be explained by the inadequacy of institutions and the persistence of a certain cavalier insouciance about the facts. Detailed information was wanted now and on time with almost the same concern expended on the receipt of tax money in the right amount and on time. And when the accounts were being kept they were to be kept in such a way that it would be a relatively simple matter for the Deputation to follow the execution of the contribution system. In the enthusiasm for a running account of tax receipts the authors of the Instructions went so far as to propose the creation of an office of War Comptroller and to fill it with a man who had the training for the post, training that included a knowledge of double entry bookkeeping. This bookkeeping *"mercantili stylo"* might serve to characterize the attitude as a whole that expressed itself in a manner that would have found favor in any advanced commercial establishment or any well-run estate. Even the highly sacral monarchy of the Habsburgs could no longer do without the most modern of financial conveniences or virtues -- thrift, industry, thoroughness -- that sounded the advent of a new epoch.

It would be an intriguing, if pointless, exercise to search out the origins of the characteristically Austrian expression of this modernity. Austrian cameralism suggests a possible connecting link between advanced notions of administration and their statement in this particular context. But in the absence of any certain clues it would seem wiser to suspect that the new style owed more to imitation and to inspired common sense than to the writings of Becher, Schröder, and Hornigk. That these men had contributed to the establishment in Austria of new techniques and new expectations cannot be questioned but that they stood as godfathers to what was said in the Instructions remains very doubtful indeed.

The elaborate and significant character of this document served to provide the new Deputation with enormous responsibilities and, at the same time, to reduce its freedom of movement. It was a highly self-conscious step in the direction of reform in administration and in the internal consistency of the Monarchy, a new departure that was to take place under the contrasting auspices of the patriarchal and the rationalistic modes of thought. The emphasis placed on Hungary was such as to raise serious doubts about the ability of the Deputation to have anything in the way of success. But even more critical for its success or failure was the age, the personal idiosyncrasies, the prejudices, the health of those who had been called by the Emperor to participate in this "so important work" on which so much of the security and the well-being of the lands and peoples of the House of Austria depended.

Notes

1. The "Ordnung und Instruction" has been published in FellnerKretschmayr, *Die österreichische Zentralverwaltung* (Veröffentlichungen der Kommission für neuere Geschichte Österreichs, 7), Abt. I, Bd. III, 24-38.

2. "Conferentz, den 21. Augusti 1696," Vorträge, XXXVI (1696 VIII-XII), 194-196.

3. Members present included Dietrichstein, Kinsky, Starhemberg, Breuner, Bucceleni (the last four *ex officio* members of the Deputation when it came into being) and the *referendarii* Mayr, Weber, Bechin, and Palm, *ibid.*, 194.

4. "De 4 millionibus nihil vellet regnum audire.", *ibid.*, 194.

5. "Conferentia, den 28, Augusti 1696," *ibid.*, 196-198.

6. "Betreffend die accisen suadere non posset, dass certum pro incerto fabren zu lassen.", *ibid.*, 196.

7. In a "Conferentz, den 9. Octobris 1696, in puncto der accisen," there is a record of the interchange": Celsissimus Princeps putaret, besser zu sein, dass die Canzleyen immediate die subiecta hieher begehrten, und nicht per gubernium. Male habuit dominus Kinsky: Der Fürst müesse reden, was händ und fües habe. Er sage ja, das er die leuth nicht kenne. Hoc graviter sensit Princeps: Ess habe ja händ und füess. Sie verlangten und wolten ia auf diese weiss bey keiner conferentz mehr sein.", *ibid.*, 201.

8. "Dietrichstein: "Einer aus Schlesien habe ein proiect eines viehaufschlags, für gewis s von 12 millionen."; then in cipher the secretary wrote: "Risit d(ominus) Kinski.", "Conferentia, den 14. Augusti 1696," *ibid.*, 194.

9. Kollonich' a remarks were made in the course of a conference that has no date; the protocol begins in the middle of the conference. "Dominus Cardinalis: Er hette die verandtwortung aller seelen' hoc in Ungaria, quod pontifex in christianitate, et primas regni... Man wolle scepter und cronen sambt der christenheit in gefahr setzten... Er khönne auff Rom gehen, ibi haberet a Pontifice 4.000 et a Rege Hispaniarum 6.000 cronen.... Er seye ihme nicht gescheid genueg. Die Conferentz habe es auff ihr gewissen, wan sie es Ihr. May. nicht vortrage.", *ibid.*, 192.

10. "Ungari dedissent 4,644.000 fl. Siebenbürgen habe sehr viel über die 400.000 fl. geben.... Von denen ländern seind nur 7 zu hoffen, 4 millionen aus Hungarn, 1 million aus Sibenbürgen. Ein jeder werde das eüsserste thuen"; earlier in his *votum* he had said: "Sub ipsius praesidio Camerae ostensum esset, dass man mit 10 million erklecken könne; darüber wire man aufgesprungen.", the conference of Sept. 20, 1697, *ibid.* (Mappe 1697), 83-84.

11. "Quia ordinaria non sufficerent, auff die accisen zu reflectiren. Ante annum zu

arbeiten angefangen. Parum autem factum. Würde nicht untheuenlich sein, aus denen länderen erfahrne leuth darzu zu nemmen und hieher zu berueffen.... Ausszuarbeithen. Die cantzleyen und stellen solten darzuethun.... Bey der Cammer, bey dem Proviantambt, bey dem Commissariatambt zu sehen, wie man helffen könne. Ihr. May. könten es allein nicht richten; man müesse ihnen an die hand geben. Wisse weiter nichts zu sagen. Man solle dass werckh mit ernst angreiffen.", "Conferentia, den 28. Augusti 1696, bey hoff...", *ibid.*, (Mappe 1696 VIII-XII), 198.

12. *Feldzüge des Prinzen Eugen von Savoyen* (Vienna, 1876), Ser. I,
Bd. I, 276-283 (with a number of tables illustrating the provisions of the various ordinances.

13. The conference ran for two days, Sept. 19 and 20, 1697, Vorträge, XXXVI (Mappe 1697), 73-84.

14. Kinsky: "Die länder hätten keinen schuz und auch keine ausrichtung. Recurrerent ad Consilium Bellicum, sed nullimi responsum exspectaret, an non fuerint insultus. Das proiect examinirt. Wan ein anderer die einkünfte besser austheilen könnte und mehr wisse, müesse er selbe zeigen.... Sicut omne principitum grave, ita (followed by "sicut" crossed out) etiam hic.", *ibid.*, 74-75.

15. "Der alte fues aber habe gleichwohl denen ländern wohl bekomben.
Putaret, dass es vol darbey bleiben solte.", *ibid.*, 76.

16. "Stahrnberg laudat votum des Mansfeld.... Schimpflich, dass man
nach der victori einen misscredit in die obristen sezen wolte.... Der graf Khinsky wäre übl informirt, wan er meldet, dass der Hofkriesgrath die scahen ligen lasse. Solle sich die insinuata vorbringen lassen, diese würden ein mehrers zeigen.", *ibid.*, 79-80.

17. "Haben wir mis schon in unserm dieser deputation und ihrer
bestellung halber jüngsthin umterm dat den 24. Novembris erlassenen decret des mehrern und deutlich dahin vernehmen lassen, was die ursach seie, so uns zu dieser verordnung bewogen haben...", Fellner-Kretschmayr, *op. cit.* Abt. I, Bd. III, 24.

18. Leopold to Kinsky, Vienna, Nov. 25, 1697, Grosse Korrespondenz,
LXIII, #2, 870-873, which contains the remark, '...ut tu praefatae Deputationi non soltun adsis, sed etiam ut praeses dirigas...".

19. The following section is based entirely on the document in FellnerKretschmayr, *op. cit.*, Abt. I, Bd. I, 24-38.

20. "...weil der nervus aller geschäfte welche diser deputation obligen
und worauf das gauze werk beruhet, auf die geldmittel, folglich auf die 12 millionen...", *ibid.*, 27.

21. The usual schedule of payments is described in A. Wolf, "Die Hofkammer under Kaiser Leopold I," *Sitzungsberichte der Philosophisch-historischen Classe der Kais. Akadamie der Wissenschaften*, XI (1853), #1, 456. For an indication of the actual rate of contribution, cf. Fellner-Kretschmayr, *op. cit.*, Abt. I, Bd. I, 27n.

Chapter Four
Praesentibus / Committeemen

"...von unsern hofcanzleien, hofkriegsrath, hofcammer und generalkriegscomrnissariatsambt zusambengesetzte deputation..."
Ordnung und Instruction

Committeemen[1] :

- Chairman (Praeses)

1. Count Franz Ulrich Kinsky (1634-1699)
2. Count Ferdinand Bonaventura Harrach (1637-1706), appointed March 9, 1699

- The Members

I. Court Chancelleries
A. Imperial Court Chancellery
1. Count Dominik Andreas Kaunitz (1655-1705) - Imperial Chancellor, Jan. 8, 1698 - Jan. 11, 1705.

B. Austrian Court Chancellery
1. Count Julius Friedrich Bucceleni (? - 1712) - Austrian Court Chancellor, Feb. 13, 1694 - June 3, 1705.

C. Bohemian Court Chancellery
1. Count Franz Ulrich Kinsky (1634-1699) - Supreme Bohemian Chancellor, April 8, 1683 - Feb. 28, 1705.
2. Count Johann Franz Wrbna (1634-1705) - Supreme Bohemian

Chancellor, March 12, 1700 - June 6, 1705.

II. War Council
1. Count Ernst Rüdiger Starhemberg (1638-1701) - President, War Council, Jan. 29, 1692 - Jan. 4, 1701.
2. Count Heinrich Franz Mansfeld (1640-1715), Prince of Fondi - President, War Council, July 27, 1701 - June 28, 1703.

III. Treasury
1. Count Seyfried Christoph Breuner (? - 1698) - President of the Treasury, Oct. 26, 1694 - May 11, 1698.
2. Count Gundacker Thomas Starhemberg (1663-1745) - Vice-Pres., Director, Aug. 18, 1698 - Dec. 10, 1700.
3. Count Gotthard Heinrich Salaburg - President of the Treasury, Dec. 10, 1700 - June (?) 1703.

IV. General War Commissariat
1. Count Max Ludwig Breuner (11643-1716) - General War Commissar, ? - 1705.
2. Count Leopold Cardinal Kollonich (1631-1707) - Prince-Primate of Hungary, 1695-1707.

V. Referendare
1. Johann David Palm - The Treasury
2. Augustin Thomas Wöbern (Webern) - The War Council
3. Mayer
4. Bein
5. The Secretary

* * *

The Instructions devoted relatively little time to the crucial question of the Deputation's membership. The decree which had preceded them and which had had the honor of being the first to announce the establishment of the Deputation may possibly have gone into this subject at some length, but in the second and more detailed statement the point was simply and apparently unambiguously made that it was to consist of the "court chancelleries, the War Council, the Treasury, and the General War Commissariat." [2]   This brevity made good sense at so early a point in the organization of a new administrative group, and brevity provided the Emperor with a chance to be somewhat flexible in choosing the men who were to join it. The important thing that operated here was not so much individuals as the official agencies that were to participate; once they had been formally invited to join the Deputation it would be time to consider appointments on an individual basis.

The formula was not, however, without its ambiguities. For when the Emperor spoke of the "court chancelleries" one could assume that he was referring to the Austrian and the Bohemian Chancelleries. The chiefs of those offices were bound to be present as a matter of course, but it was not at all clear whether Hungary's Chancellor would be represented or whether the Imperial Vice-chancellor was to represent the Imperial Court Chancellery. The practice suggested that it would be unlikely for a Hungarian to take a seat in so select and authoritative a committee of the Austrian1 central administration, and the Hungarian Chancellor could not be regarded as coming even close to the prestige invested in the Austrian and Bohemian Chancellors. The question of Hungarian representation could not be solved by providing the Hungarians with no spokesman at all, and a solution of sorts was found by asking the Prince-Primate of Hungary to serve in the Deputation. The irrepressible Cardinal Kollonich hardly figured as a devoted exponent of the Hungarians' opinions, but such was the dignity of his ecclesiastical office and its influence in the Hungarian constitutional system that the Hungarians could not complain too violently that they had been overlooked. The question of representation from the Imperial Court Chancellery, an office whose work was almost exclusively concerned with Imperial, that is German, rather than Austrian affairs, was finally decided in favor of participation. This decision may have been based not so much on the office itself and what it represented within the official hierarchy at the Court of Vienna but on the need for having the man who had just assumed the post of Imperial Vice-chancellor present at the deliberations of the Deputation. For Count Dominik Andreas Kaunitz had been rising steadily in the Emperor's favor, and his talents as a diplomat might be of some use in discussions that concerned the rivalries of the chief agencies of the government. The fact that his own office was not immediately concerned with Austrian affairs made it likely that he would have sufficient detachment to be able to contribute to the formation of a consensus view. Kaunitz had the additional merit that he made a good replacement for an ailing or disinterested Chairman of the Deputation. During the time that Kinsky presided over the destinies of the Deputation he had less to do, but with the death of Kinsky and the appointment of Harrach to succeed him Kaunitz soon established himself as one of the more active and vocal members, an indication of what a wise move it had been to appoint him in the first place.

The committee roster at its greatest extension included the following dignitaries: the Imperial Vice-chancellor, the Austrian Court Chancellor, the Supreme Bohemian Chancellor, the President of the Treasury, the President of the War Council, the General War Commissar, and the Prince-Primate of Hungary. In addition there were the *Referendare*, the top professional bureaucrats, from the various agencies represented. Anonymity covered much of their activity as one might expect. They were present to lend support to the statements expressed by their superiors, to present their own views, and to keep minutes of the meetings which would be used by their particular office in keeping a close watch on decisions made in the Deputation. No one could envy a group of men who were required to take a secondary place and who were often better informed and more aware of day to day business than the grandees they attended. Some hint of their mentality and general outlook can be found in the protocols of the Deputation, for the irrepressible Secretary who kept them did not conceal his impatience with the proceedings and his criticism of individual members.

If the Instructions had not given much attention to the question of the membership they were even more discreet in discussing the role of the Chairman. Certainly it was in the very nature of this new committee that its Chairman would have a preponderant influence on its work. Without the kind of leadership that only a vigorous and imaginative Chairman could provide, the meetings might easily descend to the level of constant bickering and name-calling. Since the Deputation was not an office and had no permanent staff or chancellery, the chief responsibility for keeping the group together devolved upon one man -- the Chairman. And he had to be someone with a modicum of talent for administration as well as a man who had a large degree of influence with the Emperor. The most efficient of committees would have been reduced to complete ineffectiveness if its leader had not been able to insure that the decisions it made would be officially approved and supported by the Emperor; only that kind of confidence gave any hope at all that the work of the Deputation would be crowned with some success.

At the more mundane level of committee business the Chairman had to make sure that the meetings followed the schedule laid down in the Instructions, though he could, if he felt that there was insufficient business, make exceptions to this rule. It was responsibility to prepare the agendas, to see to it that there was a full representation at the meetings, to provide some direction during the discussion itself, to state the findings by way of a conclusion, and then to take charge of reporting this in person or in writing to the Emperor. Within these limits the Chairman retained a good deal of freedom of action, and he could, if he wished to do so, impress his personality on the committee as a whole. But this position of leadership, of molding the Deputation in its expression of its official opinion, did not extend to an outright tyranny over the members who were not at all ready to be told what they must do and who were prepared, if they felt it was necessary, to make their case known to the Emperor. For they reserved the right to continue the discussion outside the meetings and to do this in the face of the hope that a decision which was once reached in the Deputation would be final so far as its particular area of activity was concerned. The Instructions had made it perfectly clear that there would be issues on which it would be impossible to establish a consensus, and the fact that the whole matter was then referred to the Emperor made for good sense in an administrative way but for additional confusion as far as the wavering temperament of Leopold was concerned. The position of Chairman carried with it one of the most important and unattractive responsibilities in the Austrian governmental system, and no one could be at all surprised that Kinsky had at first been reluctant to serve as the Chairman.

Since this gifted and somewhat perplexing man was to play so central a role in the early history of the Deputation he deserves a somewhat more extended description than that accorded to the other members. Kinsky stood out because he happened to be the Chairman but also because the quality of his mind and his general political acumen were far in advance of most of his colleagues. His background, his education, his experience as a member of the Imperial service had given him a sophistication, a subtlety that was virtually unique at the Court of Vienna. The scion of a great noble family of Bohemia, he knew what it was to be regarded with some suspicion as a descendant of rebels against Habsburg rule and, at the same time, to be thought of as a most uncompromising servant of dynastic rather than of Bohemian interests. These suspicions, which hardly did justice to the nuance of his position, did have some slight foundation in fact. The Kinsky name had been closely associated with the Bohemian uprising that had found its conclusion at the debacle of the White Mountain, and an uncle of Franz Ulrich had lost his life because of his loyalty to the great Wallenstein. With that wonderful resilience that so often crops up in aristocratic circles the Kinsky clan had recovered rather quickly from its lack of political judgment during the rebellion and the war that followed and in our Kinsky's generation the accent rested heavily on complete loyalty to the dynasty and to a reluctance to pursue individual or regional interests. The Bohemians did feel disappointed at times that their chief spokesman in Vienna, their Supreme Bohemian Chancellor, made so little apparent effort to defend and preserve their somewhat circumscribed liberties and privileges (they were so often one and the same thing).

Popular prejudice might well feel uncomfortable and uncertain of itself in the presence of a man who did not simply express the views current in his class or circle. Kinsky had real subtlety of mind, and he had the further advantage of education abroad which in his case must have been more than perfunctory. Certainly, by the time he had reached a position of sufficient eminence in the Imperial service to be one of the Austrian representatives at the Congress of Nimwegen he so managed to impress the French that they spoke admiringly of his *"penetration."* The use of the phrase had a patronizing ring to it, but the French were discerning observers of European statesmen and diplomats, and their favorable impression of Kinsky would receive later confirmation at the hands of the equally discerning Venetians. These early years developed Kinsky's interest in and talent for foreign affairs, and even though he was to spend a good part of his life in situations where he was expected to devote himself to domestic affairs -- his long service as Supreme Bohemian Chancellor was a case in point -- his refusal to become parochial in his outlook and to withdraw from his involvement in Austria's relations with its friends and foes was pronounced. In the years that followed the siege of Vienna Kinsky became Austria's acknowledged expert on Turkish affairs. This fit in with his support of the Austrian party at Court and allowed him to have some honorable part in the achievement of a general peace for southeastern Europe in 1699, the Peace of Carlowitz that was concluded a month before his death.

His appointment as the Chairman of the Deputation represented the last great vote of confidence he was to receive from the Emperor, for Kinsky without being entirely aware of it had reached the zenith of his power and influence in the final weeks of 1697. The way to the final honor of an appointment as Lord High Steward seemed open, and there was no real competition that might set a limit to his power and influence as Stratmann had done until his death in 1693. Appearances suggested that he had become Leopold's chief minister; certainly they collaborated closely, and few decisions were made without consulting Kinsky. But his chance to reign supreme was to be mercilessly brief. For one thing, his health began to deteriorate, and that penance of so many statesman of the day, the gout, made it increasingly difficult for him to attend meetings and to maintain the kind of daily contact on which so much depends. He had always been known for his irritability and for what seemed to be a perfect gift for establishing lifelong enmities. This explained the curious situation in which a number of the key officials and the chief foreign diplomats refused to have much to do with him; they all remembered occasions on which they felt they had suffered at his hands. Illness only developed this tendency and made of it an important factor in the daily business of the Deputation.

But the great blow to his pride and his ambition that was to result in a growing disenchantment with affairs in general and with the work of the Deputation in particular came from the Emperor's decision to display his enthusiasm for Count Ferdinand Bonaventure Harrach. Harrach, recently returned from an unsuccessful embassy to Spain, had been received with open arms by his friend the Emperor who thought it only natural to appoint this accomplished courtier as the successor to Prince Dietrichstein in the post of Lord High Steward of the Court. The actual appointment took place shortly before Kinsky's death on February 28, 1699, but the sick and increasingly bitter runner-up for the affections of the Emperor must have realized that he was to be deprived of this final accolade. It was not that Leopold did not admire him and consider him to be a most valuable collaborator, but he could not hide the fact that at certain moments he preferred the easygoing Harrach to the prickly Kinsky. At the very end of the latter's life the Emperor composed something of an epitaph with his own hand on a page that was inserted in their correspondence. His last letter to Kinsky had concluded with the words: "Farewell, my Kinsky," and whether he knew that this was to be the final farewell it had to serve that purpose. The epitaph consisted of the sign of the cross and beneath it these words: "Rest in peace, worthy man. You shall embody the deepest longing of an unworthy posterity."[4]

It was only natural that with Kinsky gone Harrach should succeed him as Chairman of the Deputation.[5] The choice could not have been otherwise; there was no one else with the possible exception of Kaunitz who had sufficient influence to qualify for the job. But Harrach could hardly follow in Kinsky's wake. He had neither the same amount of talent nor the same capacity for work. His experience as an administrator did not suggest that he would be an active participant, and this in fact proved to be the case. Though he remained as the nominal head of the operation he appears only infrequently in the protocols, and whatever he might have contributed was lost due to his striking lack of interest. Harrach was a man wholly without ambition. Thanks to the eminence of his name, the family wealth, and the closeness of his relations with the Emperor he did not need ambition as lesser men did to find their way to positions of power and influence. The unfortunate consequence of this lack of ambition, where the Deputation was concerned, was that it was deprived of effective leadership at a time when it needed it the most. The Deputation did survive many blows, but there is good reason to believe that it never entirely recovered from the death of its first Chairman.

The man who managed in some degree to make up for Harrach's evident lack of concern was Count Dominik Andreas Kaunitz.[6] He had already served as an acting Chairman when Kinsky had been ill or had been otherwise prevented from attending a meeting, and it was logical that he would continue to serve in the same capacity under Harrach. Kaunitz and Kinsky had much in common. They both were members of the Bohemian nobility, and Kaunitz, like Kinsky, made his reputation first as an Austrian negotiator at a peace congress. His fame was the more recent, for he had barely returned from his triumph at the Congress of Ryswick before he was asked to join the Deputation. Though his horizons were presumably as broad as Kinsky's he fell short of the older man's claim to distinction as a student (and practitioner) of European power politics. But what he lacked in sheer intelligence and energy he made up with personal charm and an unfailing desire to please, and those who had to treat with him as an Acting Chairman would find him conspicuously less anxious to create difficult situations and rather less inclined to explore all of the consequences of any projected official action.

In so far as Kaunitz might be said to follow a line in domestic politics he was a member of the "Bohemian party." That is he combined a professional loyalty to the Emperor and the views current among his ministers, views that inclined to tightening the hold of the central government on the country, with an attachment to the more restricted perspectives of the average Bohemian magnate. Kaunitz could in a moment of crisis for the Monarchy leave Vienna and go off to look after his estates, and though such conduct was found reprehensible by Prince Eugene it did not cause much comment on the part of other ministers who had similar inclinations.[7] Kaunitz was thought to be accessible to those who were willing to give him presents, but such conduct did not set him apart from the generality of public officials at the time. Those who might wonder at his growing influence -- he alone appeared to be the natural successor to Kinsky -- often inclined to the belief that he owed his rise to the evident charms of his wife; she had been born a Sternberg and had married a Wratislaw before her marriage to Kaunitz. Perhaps the essence of his problem was that he fell between two vastly different generations of Austrian ministers. He was at least twenty years younger than most of the members of the Deputation, and, on the other hand, he was older than the great quadrumvirate of the reign of Joseph I: Eugene of Savoy, Gundacker Starhemberg, Johann Wenzel Wratislaw, and Philipp Sinzendorf. While many of his opinions on the great questions of the day and the need for reform of the Austrian system often approximated theirs, yet he could not bring himself whether out of calculation or a lack of energy to become a committed "young Turk," and on more than one occasion he was to place himself squarely behind the old guard that refused to make way for more talented youth. In the end he fell short of the zenith which Kinsky had reached. Though he did much to bring about the changes in the ministry in 1703 that opened the way to the younger generation he could not enjoy the radically changed situation. Death came to him in 1705 at the relatively youthful age of fifty. It would be left to his far more gifted grandson Prince Wenzel Eusebius Kaunitz to reach the position which Dominik Andreas had so clearly desired.

Kinsky, Harrach, and Kaunitz shared the chief responsibility for the work of the Deputation in a curiously uneven way. Kinsky did too much; Harrach did too little, and Kaunitz tried as best he could to keep the committee in motion. Kaunitz in his capacity as a member of the Bohemian noble order had his definite interests at stake in the work of the Deputation, and he would not be at all backward in stating what could be described as the views of the Bohemian party. But his own official responsibilities were largely concerned with foreign affairs, and even as an Imperial Vice Chancellor he showed far less interest in the workings of that chancellery than did his predecessors or his successor, the busy Count Schönborn.

If the situation of the Chairman could be said to be a regular one only during the first months of Kinsky's sway the quality of the members of the Deputation was far less erratic. They were for the most part men who had a long experience of Austrian governmental affairs, and they had carried the anonymity which this could often encourage in the not particularly gifted servants of the Emperor to a high degree of development. Starhemberg continued to trail clouds of glory, and Kollonich never failed to bring his absolutely unique views on a variety of subjects to the fore. But the general impression of the mere committee members was that of men without the gifts of a Kinsky or the charm of a Harrach. They had seniority and longevity and not a few could look back to an early personal association with the Emperor, but when it came to the quality of their contribution to the work of a committee such as this, it would not be too much to say that it went far to confirming the pessimistic views of the men of the Emperor's generation that were held by the men who gravitated to his son and heir Joseph.

A man like Count Julius Friedrich Bucceleni was a perfect example of the strengths and the limitations of the older generation of Austrian ministers.[8] The Buccelenis were relative latecomers to this intensely aristocratic world, and though there was the persistent belief that they descended from an old noble family of Lorraine the truth of the matter seemed to be that they came originally from Inner Austria, from Carniola to be precise. A Bucceleni had been a close collaborator of Hans Eggenburg, the great favorite of Emperor Ferdinand II, and Count Horaz Bucceleni, the father of Julius Friedrich, had seen many years of service in the *Regiment*, the local administration, of Lower Austria and had acquired along the way a reputation as a "very pious lord and a great zealot for the Catholic religion."[9] The son had begun life as a member of the *Ritterstand* but thanks to long years of service in the *Regiment* and in the Court Chancellery ended his life as a Count of the Holy Roman Empire. He it was who had succeeded Theodor Althet Stratmann as Court Chancellor, and though he seems to have inherited his predecessor's antipathy to Kinsky he had no hope of actively competing with him. He was less of a distinct individual than a member of a type of Austrian administrators: earnest, just, kind to the poor, grave and verbose in their expression of their views and in the conduct of their office, a member of the aristocratic order without being an aristocrat in spirit. His position in the Deputation was an immensely sensitive one, yet apart from an occasional clash with Kinsky or he contented himself to a great degree with frank confessions of ignorance, the statement of facts too well known to bear repetition, and gloomy predictions about the future that were hardly calculated to have much effect on men who had become progressively inured to prophecies of doom. In Bucceleni's hands the Austrian Court Chancellery had lost its place at the head of the movement to reform and to modernize and had tended to relapse into a querulous defense of its own bailiwick. This loss in political energy and in forward motion did not fail to have important consequences, too, for the Deputation; the weakening of any part of the committee's component parts meant a weakening of its ability to handle the complex relationships of the political, financial, and military establishments in the Austrian Monarchy.

The President of the Treasury, Count Seyfried Christof Breuner, had much in common with Bucceleni.[10] He, too, had reached his presidency only after long years of subaltern status, and he probably owed his high office to sheer personal and political survival rather than to any pronounced talent for finance. The Breuners did have a great reputation as Imperial officials and as Presidents of the Treasury. A Philipp Breuner had been one of the first to preside over the Treasury in the reign of Ferdinand I, and his branch of the family had continued to do its part with each generation producing one or more devoted public servants. The Styrian branch of the family had proved to be the more exciting and influential one at time -- Count Jacob Breuner had been a chief minister of Rudolf II and his sons had been active in the Treasury

-- but their Lower Austrian cousins had greater staying power and a more living tradition of service. Seyfried Christof had been a Treasury Councillor as early as 1671, an indication that he was approaching the customary end of his official service when he was called to sit in the Deputation. His contribution to the Deputation was to suffer from the fact that by the time it had been organized and had begun to have regular sessions Count Breuner's illness forced him to ask the Emperor to allow the young Gundacker Starhemberg to attend the meetings in his place.[11] Breuner's death on May 8, 1698 brought an end to a long career in Austrian administration that induded the briefest of encounters with the history of the Deputation.

The Breuner name and tradition were to continue there thanks to the official presence of a Breuner cousin, Count Max Ludwig Breuner, then the General War Commissar.[12] Max Ludwig had a military rather than bureaucratic background, and though family ties may have moved him to a greater measure of collaboration with the Treasury his own training and instincts made him view the office he directed as an appendage of the War Council. Slightly younger than most of the committee members, he had no qualms about which generation he would support: he came to be regarded as a close friend and collaborator of men like Count Mansfeld, whom Eugene of Savoy regarded as particular obstacles in the way of a reform of the Austrian administration and especially the War Office. Max Ludwig Breuner had staying power at any rate; he survived the great change of ministers in 1703 and was required to retire from his office only at the death of Leopold I in 1705. His successor at that time was the renowned Austrian negotiator at Carlowitz Count Leopold Schlick whose military exploits ran well behind his capabilities as a master intriguer at Court.

The Breuners were not the only clan to have contributed more than one of its members to the roster of the Deputation; the Starhembergs were equally well represented. Count Ernst Rüdiger Starhembeing was the President of the War Council at the time, and his younger half brother Gundacker served as a member in the period that he was the temporary head of the Treasury, August 1698 to December 1700. The Starhembergs had the best of hereditary claims to such representation, for they belonged to that most exclusive circle of Austrian noble families, the *Landesaposteln*, that went back to the Babenberg rule in Austria.[13] As such they could in their more nostalgic moments look upon the House of Austria as newcomers, and they continued to make good the family claim to participate in the central government and in the government of Lower Austria. No important public activity was quite complete without the presence of at least one of the members of a family that had by now produced innumerable branches and lines. The family had reason to be pleased that two of its members were men of such influence in the Austrian administration and were to play a far from negligible role in the work of the Deputation.

The older Starhemberg was very much the soldier, rough and bluff and insensitive to other points of view.[14] He had experienced his greatest moment during the siege of Vienna, when he had directed the defense of the beleaguered city against the Turks. Ever after that he had been seen through the clouds of glory that surrounded that courageous performance, and only those who observed him more closely had reason to believe that this heroic life contained moments that were not so certifiably glorious. For the truth was that the aging general did not win any laurels as a chief of the War Council. He did manage to express the military point of view with his characteristic candor, but he could do little to defend the army's special interests by working for greater cooperation with the chancelleries and the Treasury. By the beginning of 1698 his health had begun to decline and he increasingly took refuge in his own amusements, the traditional leisure activities of the great aristocrat, hunting and the maintenance of a fine stable. His absences from the Deputation increased in proportion, and it became something of a mystery as to whether or not he absented himself from disinterest or out of pique that his views did not receive the respectful attention he thought they deserved But even if he had been more loyal in his attendance it was difficult to see what he could have done to change the general line of Deputation policy; for all the golden aureole that surrounded his name Ernst Rüdiger remained basically an "*honnête homme* with circumscribed views."[15]

Gundacker Starhemberg had far more claim to originality and in his own way he was the most promising member of the Deputation in its early period of formation.[16] He could not have differed more from the conventional figure of the hero who happened to be his brother. In his youth he had been prepared for an ecclesiastical career and had found a good living in the Cathedral Chapter of Olomouc before deciding to exchange that pious and not very exciting life for the more challenging one of public service. In a fairly brief time he managed to secure a reputation as an expert on government finance, a reputation that did not come easily to the born aristocrat. Even the few bankers in the country respected this Starhemberg's surefootedness as he made his way through the veritable maze of contributions and anticipations (government loans) that he would strive so continuously and fruitlessly to simplify. His talent was unquestioned; his loyalty to the House of Austria proven on a number of occasions, and he alone of the members of the Deputation was to survive into the reign of Maria Theresa and to earn her gratitude for his selfless service to the dynasty. But in 1698 he still had the fatal imperfection of youth, and though he had more acknowledged talent than the man he temporarily replaced and the man who succeeded him, Count Gotthard Salaburg, he had to be content with an interim appointment. The Emperor presumably felt that even this talent would require some years of experience before it could be trusted with full powers at the Treasury.

This Starhemberg suffered from a lack of diplomatic experience and a certain insensitivity to the chief problems in the field of Austrian internal politics. It was not that he was completely bereft of good sense in such matters, but he could not be expected to combine an already massive reputation in connection with the Imperial finances and a certain command of all the other major areas of governmental activity. His youth and lack of experience encouraged him to adopt positions that could not fail to distress the older generation. They shook their heads at the impertinence of a young man who appeared to believe that something could be done to remedy the situation that faced the Deputation. Because he had the welfare of the Monarchy and the good order of the Treasury so much at heart, he could look beyond the iron limits of custom to a really thoroughgoing system of income tax and to an arrangement of long-term credits from the various diets that would allow the planners in Vienna far more freedom of action. Beyond this level of generalization Gundacker Starhemberg did not go. Though he had ideas, he claimed no originality for them nor could he do so, and they were never developed or set down in a logical form. It was his well-founded sense of urgency, based on his incomparable grasp of the depth of the financial crisis, that made him almost against his will a proponent of more powerful and innovative government at the heart of the Monarchy.

Gundacker Starhemberg had begun lift as a cleric and ended it as an expert on finance. Leopold Cardinal Kollonich began life as a soldier, albeit a member of the Knights of Malta, and ended it as the chief ecclesiastical officer of Hungary and as a fixture in the Privy Conference and the Deputation.[17] The quality of heroism that he had exhibited as a youthful knight persisted even when he appeared to be exclusively devoted to works of religion and of charity. During the siege of Vienna he showed his basic courage and refusal to take advantage of the inevitable excuses for leaving the city so soon to come under attack. He held his ground and did much to maintain the morale of the inhabitants, and this presence in the city probably did more than anything else to assure him the gratitude and the respect of the Emperor. The emotional world of the crusader presented no problems for the erstwhile knight, and while he went about the business of collecting episcopal sees and appointments in the Hungarian Treasury and in the Treasury in Vienna -- for a time he served as the President of the Treasury -- he never lost the quality of complete and utter devotion to a cause that had already begun to reveal incipient signs of old age. When he thought of the Turk, he responded without nuance and hesitation: this was the Infidel who must be driven out of Europe, and when he thought of the Protestants the aversion he experienced was only slightly less than that which he reserved for the Moslem.

No one could deny that he faced a particularly difficult task in acting as a "representative" of Hungary in the Deputation. The family of which he was a member was of Croatian origin. Thanks to the advance of the Turks it had taken refuge in the Austrian and Hungarian borderlands without managing to acclimate itself entirely to Hungarian society and culture. The very presence of such a man in the post of Primate of Hungary testified to a growing uncertainty in official circles about the undivided loyalty of a prelate of impeccably Hungarian background. Men like Szelepcsényi and Széchényi served the work of restoring Catholicism in Hungary with great enthusiasm, but when it came to overlooking the constitutional traditions of the country and their own significant role in Hungarian affairs they were much less pliable. Kollonich made no secret of the fact that he served the Emperor without any ambivalence or reservations; the question of his suitability as a spokesman for the Hungarians was more complex. Even if it would be unwise to dismiss him simply as an alien influence that had little or nothing to do with the best interests of the Hungarian nation a case could be made (on the basis of his statements in the Deputation) for the view that the Primate of the Hungarians often erred in his judgment of what the Kingdom of St. Stephen could be expected to do in the way of taxation. His roseate view of the ability to pay the contribution of four million gulden did more honor to his enthusiastic nature than to any sober assessment of the actual conditions in his subsection of Catholic Christendom.

These men with the more shadowy figures of the *Referendare*, the departmental experts who had little to say but who constituted the best source of dependable information on any of the questions touched upon by the Deputation, comprised the initial group of committee members. By 1701 a number of important vacancies had occurred that brought new men into the Deputation. Perhaps the most striking of these was Count Heinrich Mansfeld who succeeded to the post of President of the War Council on the death of Ernst Rüdiger Starhemberg.[18] Mansfeld had been a close friend of his predecessor, and he rejoiced in quite as close a relationship with the Emperor, so it was not at all surprising that he was chosen in place of the gifted Eugene of Savoy. Mansfeld was more familiar, more predictable, and he did not suffer from an excess of talent. His administration of the War Council did not represent an impressive chapter in its history, and the disappointed Eugene was not alone in complaining that a man so bereft of military gifts and administrative talent had been chosen to preside over the military establishment in the midst of wartime.

Mansfeld made no secret of his uncompromising support of a conservative approach to all of Austria's problems, foreign and domestic, and in this he found a natural ally in Count Gotthard Salaburg, another old crony of Leopold I.[19] Salaburg represented the single most disastrous appointment of Leopold's last years. Though he could not be accused of gross misuse of government funds like Count Georg Sinzendorf, he did little more than add confusion to the already overstrained efforts of the Treasury. The interregnum in which Gundacker Starhemberg had done what he could to improve matters had not been long enough, and with men like Mansfeld, Salaburg, and Bucceleni in the most critical posts the worst qualities of the Leopoldinian system had their final heyday. Kinsky was followed as Supreme Bohemian Chancellor by Count Johann Franz Wrbna who does not appear to have taken a very active part in the work of the Deputation.[20] He had had a distinguished career as a public servant, but he, too, was approaching its final moments when he was called upon to join the Deputation.

Even the most superficial acquaintance with these men does not fail to produce a characteristic resonance of its own. Though they differed to some extent in their personal styles, though they were known to have developed longstanding antipathies for one another -- the enmity of Kinsky and Starhemberg was only one of the more striking examples of this taste for competition -- they still presented a strikingly homogeneous picture. The average age of the members of the Deputation was over sixty, and a fair number were within a few years of the end of their careers. Sickness and a growing disenchantment with public affairs did much to limit their effectiveness and to prevent them from taking as active a role as circumstances required. And when vacancies did occur and an opportunity was offered to provide the committee with new blood the Emperor ran contrary to its best interests by appointing men who were clearly inferior to the men they replaced. These gerontocrats belonged for the most part to the more sublime spheres of the Austrian and the Bohemian nobility.   Starhemberg, Breuener, and even Bucceleni had inherited claims to power in Austria; Kinsky, Kaunitz and Wrbna belonged to the inner circle of Bohemian magnates.   The Deputation thus belonged almost exclusively to the aristocratic order in society, and though the lower orders were represented by the *Referendare* official custom and the reliance on a distinction between the *Herrenstand* and the *Gelehrtenstand*, the grandees and the professional bureaucrats, meant that society's norms prevented the more informed from being heard as much as they should have been.   They were encouraged to give their *vota* at the meetings, but since they spoke at the very conclusion of the meeting and long after the chiefs of the various offices had made their opinions clear they could hardly have much impact on the sense of the meeting.   The social inequality that found itself expressed in such procedures must have been a penance for the men who had to listen attentively to the men they knew were too old and too remote from affairs to represent in an effective way the viewpoint of the chancelleries, the Treasury, or the War Council.[21]

Yet it would be a mistake to imagine that the high degree of homogeneity in age and social status precluded strong differences of views.   Loyalty to one's official responsibility often proved more crucial than a common membership in the aristocratic network that dominated Austrian society.   The blunt and unquestioning loyalty of a Starhemberg to the military viewpoint may have been more memorable, but he was only following a pattern that was weilnigh universal for all the others.   They felt deeply involved when their department came under attack or when their own conduct of its affairs received even the slightest degree of criticism.   Departmental differences of opinion did not exhaust the possibilities of division within the ranks of committeemen.   Something as basically human and as hard to control as personal antipathies also played a prominent role.   In long years of competition for the favor of the Emperor even so successful a group of aspirants to power as these men were sure to build up antagonisms that no flood of appeals for a "single mind and heart" in all they did could manage to overcome. Kinsky almost relished enmities and difficult personal situations; his long-standing contention with Starhemberg was well known, and there were moments, too, when he and Bucceleni made no secret of their lack of sympathy for one another. Perhaps the disease that most of them shared as a consequence of their aristocratic diets had something to do with this -- the prevalence of gout at so august a level hardly served the purposes of internal concord and cooperation.[22]

Even more striking than departmental differences and personal antipathies in breaking through the united front of age, aristocracy, and long experience was the presence in the committee of political views that were based on regional attachments. With the Hungarians represented somewhat ambivalently by Kollonich the Deputation was composed of men who felt a regional loyalty to Austria or to Bohemia. Though this division of feelings was far from being hard and fast in practice there could be no doubt that it was a natural and persistent concomitant of the wellnigh impregnable position of the aristocrat in Austrian government and politics. An "Austrian" and a "Bohemian" party did exist in a tentative way, and their existence was not apparent at the precise moment when the government faced the resistance of the Hungarian nobles who were not represented in the Deputation or at the higher levels of the central government. For when the Hungarians pressed their case for the preservation of their noble liberties, their Austrian and Bohemian counterparts could not pretend to be entirely unsympathetic. The impact of the Hungarian agitation as it was expressed in the inevitable memorials and in the statements of the Hungarian leaders invited to negotiate with the Deputation was felt and far from superficially. In reacting to this point of view that had some similarity to their owui the men of the Deputation revealed how dangerous it is to be certain of the significance of a term like "Habsburg absolutism." For these servants of the central authority were often of two minds, bound to support a strong and effective government and yet reluctant to undertake a reform that would weaken their own political and social power.

The contrast between the optimism of the *Ordnung und Instruction* and the atmosphere produced by the personalities of the members of the Deputation could not have been more depressing. But depressing as it was it has managed to survive with a verisimilitude that one might not have expected from a committee whose deliberations have been forgotten for so long a time. We owe this unexpected gift to the survival of the protocols of the meetings and to the mysterious and yet very lifelike Secretary who kept them.[23]

Notes

1.   The list of committeemen can make no pretension to great accuracy or completeness. It is based on information culled from the following sources: "Anhang: Verzeicbnis der Inhaber der obersten Hofwürden und der Vorstände der Zentralbehörden 1526-1749," Fellner-Kretschmayr, *Die österreichische Zentralverwaltung* (Wien, 1907), Abt. I, Bd. I, 273-288; C. von Wurzbach, *Biographisches Lexikon des Kaisertums Österreich: 1750-1850* (Wien, 1856-1891), 60 Bde.; L. Gross, *Die Geschichte der deutschen Reichshofkanzlei von 1559 bis 1806* (Inventare des Wiener Haus-, Hof- und Staatsarchivs, V) (Wien, 1933); *Beiträge zur Geschichte der niederösterreichischen Statthalterei: Die Landeschefs und Räthe dieser Behörde von 1501 bis 1896* (Wien, 1897); M. Braubach, Prinz Eugen: Eine Biographie (Wien, 1965), 5 Bde.

2.   Fellner-Kretschmayr, *op. cit.*, Abt. I, Bd. 3, 24.

3.   There is no monograph devoted to the career of Franz Ulrich Kinsky. The best brief asscssmant of his personality and his policies is to be found in H. von Srbik, *Wien und Versailles: 1692-1697* (München, 1944), 32-34.

4.   "Vale mi Khinsky....." then the sign of the cross and the words: Requiescat in pace, bonus vir -- pium desiderium scribifacis posteritatis indigna.", *Grosse Korrespondenz*, Feb. 19, 1699, fol. 1139-1140.

5.   A. Gaedeke, *Die Politik Österreichs in der Spanischen Erbfolgefrage* (Leipzig, 1877), 2 Bde., deals at great length with Harrach's embassy to Madrid; for his "Charakteristik" of Harrach, cf. I, 45-48.   Harrach first appeared at the Deputation as *"novus praeses"* on March 9, 1699, *Deputationsprotokoll* (hereafter *Dep. Prot.*) 1699, fol. 11.   His absence was frequently noted; he did not appear, for example, on either December 7 or December 10, 1699, *ibid*, fol. 68, 70.

6.   For Kaunitz, cf. L. Gross, *op. cit.*, 347-348, and the literature cited there.

7.   Braubach, *op. cit.*, II, 31-32.

8.   G. Turba, *Reichsgraf Seilern aus Ladenburg am Neckar 1646-1715* (Heidelberg, 1923), 190-191, especially Turba's view: "Bucelleni passte nicht mehr für die vielfachen Aufgaben innen- vie aussenpolitischen Monarchendienstes, vomit noch solche der Justizpflege, sogar noch finanzielle (Cameralia) und militärische (Militaria) für Inner- und Vorderösterreich verbunden waren."; *Beiträge zur Geschichte der niederösterreichischen Statthaltwrei*, 443.

9.   *Ibid.*, 439.

10.   H. Schwarz, *The Imperial Privy Council in the Seventeenth Century* (Harvard Historical Studies, LIII) (Cambridge, Mass., 1943), 208-212; *Beiträge zur Geschichte der niederösterreichischen Statthalterei*, 192-194; 226-241; Braubach, *op. cit.*, I, 267.

11. *Hoffinanz, Ungarn*, Fasz. 387, Feb. 28, 1698, fol. 316-319.

12. A. Grafen Thürheim, *Feldmarschali Ernst Rüdiger Graf Starhemberg: 1683 Wiens ruhmvoller Vertheidiger* (1638-1701) (Wien, 1882), 269; Braubach, *op. cit.* I passim, II, 24-25.

13. For Austria's *Landesaposteln*, cf. H. Schwarz, *op. cit.*, 400n.

14. A. Grafen Thurheim, *op. cit.*; T. Barker, *Double Eagle and Crescent: Vienna's Second Turkish Siege and its Historical Setting* (Albany, N. Y., 1967) ,237-240.

15. *Memoires du Duc de Villars* (The Hague, 1735), I, 304.

16. "Il... conte di Staremberg, altro ministro della "conferenza
segreta" dell'imperatore, é uomo di molto spirito e di grande penetrazione negli affari. É versatissimo nelle aziende delle finanze, ed applicato al suo officio. *Non passa pero per ministro grandemente instrutto* degli affari di stato, massimc stranieri." (italics my own)," Relazione delia Corte di Vienna del conte San Martino di Baldissero (1713)", *Relazioni di Ambasciatori Sabaudi, Genovesi e Veneti* (1693-1713), ed. Carlo Morondi (Bologna, 1935), I, 128.

17. Cardinal Kollonich has been the subject of a biography, but the book written by the Austrian church historian Joseph Maurer, *Cardinal Leopold Graf Kollonitsch, Primas von Ungarn: Sein Leben und Wirken* (Innsbruck, 1887) is less a portrait of this interesting and much neglected figure than a collection of source materials; for a brief but interesting view of the men and his work, cf. Gy. Szekfü, *Magyar törtenet* (Budapest, 1935), 243ff, Homan-Szekfü, *Magyar törtenet*, IV.

18. For a balanced and sympathetic view of a man whose talents were more courtly than military, of. A. von Arneth, *Prinz Eugen von Savoyen* (Wien, 1864) I, 204-205; also Braubach, *op. cit.*, I, 315.

19. All the authorities agree on the incompetence of Salaburg, cf. A. von Arneth, *op. cit.*, I, 205; Braubach, *op. cit.*, 315; F. von Mensi, *Die Finanzen Oesterreichs von 1701 bis 1740* (Wien, 1890), 80.

20. Braubach, *op. cit.*, II, 137.

21. For the situation of the *Referendare*, cf. L. Gross, *op. cit.*, passim. These men had positions of great responsibility, but there remained an awesome gap between the aristocrats who were the heads of the various offices and the non-noble secretaries and section chiefs. This gap can be noted in their salaries: "Breuner monatlich 900 fl; Starhemberg: 900 fl.; Palm (a *Referendar*) 90 fl.", *Dep. Prot.* 1700, fol. 176.

22. W. S. C. Copeusn in *his A Short History of the Gout and the Rheumatic Diseases* (Berkeley, 1964) has an interesting discussion of "Gout in the Seventeenth Century"

that does not dwell sufficiently on the probable political consequences of the disease, pp. 64-79.

23. For an extended discussion of the personality and views of the Secretary of the Deputation see the following chapter.

Chapter Five
Protocullum / Minutes

"Legitur protocollum..."
Deputationsprotokoll 1699

The musty bundle of documents promised all too little in the way of earthshaking revelations. It belonged to the collection of Vorträge that was preserved in Vienna's *Haus-, Hof- und Staatsarchiv* and was listed as "Faszikel 36". The Vorträge derived its name from the large numbers of reports made by Austrian ministers to the Habsburg emperors that it contained, but for the seventeenth century, for the years 1696 to 1698 in particular, it probably had little more to offer than exceedingly brief and tantalizing records of the meetings of the Privy Conference. Now since this had been the chief consultative body of Austria during the reign of Leopold I the prospect of examining its minutes had a certain initial charm, but previous fascicles had already made it quite clear that those who had taken down the record of the meetings had been quite unwilling to dispel the mystery surrounding the making of important political decisions. They did little more than note the date, the names of those present, the subject under discussion, and, on occasion, when they were in a mood for 'revelation' they might add an opinion or two, even the conclusion that had been reached. But all these single sheets told the story of a government that knew how to keep its secrets and that in doing so could only enrage those who would come searching for information in generations to come.

Yet this particular bundle did not run true to the style of those preceding it. It did contain minutes of the Privy Conference, but it also revealed the presence of a sizable booklet that did not fit in at all with the rest of the materials; it had a look and a character all its own --

somehow this interloper had made its way into the poor remains of the Privy Conference. The minute that it was opened the booklet restored one's faith and optimism. Much of it contained writing, and the entries appeared to follow a sequence that extended from the very beginning to the end. There were a number of subdivisions, as if to mark off separate meetings, and each of them bore the exciting notation, "*Sessio deput*", that is *sessio deputationis*. Since there had been a number of Austrian committees that had rejoiced in the name of '*deputatio*' it took some additional time before it became absolutely certain that this booklet contained the minutes of the meetings of the *Deputatio des Status Publico-oeconomico-militaris*. This was the *Deputationsprotokoll* for 1698, and additional investigation soon revealed that it was the first in a series of booklets and bound folios that contained committee minutes. Suddenly and quite without previous warning the history of the Deputation acquired a whole new dimension, and the way was open now to following its travail from the inside rather than from the external evidence of Imperial rescripts and decrees. Now it was possible to observe the members of the Deputation at work and to see how they went about the business of restoring order to the Emperor's administration and securing gulden for his treasury.

Everything connected with this first booklet acquired an interest of its own. Its form, the way in which it had been used, the possible identity of the individual who had taken the minutes (it was obviously the work of one man) -- all became matters of real concern. The booklet had surely been prepared with the meetings of the Deputation in mind. Sheets of the paper that was used for rough drafts by Leopold's officials had been folded into two lengthwise and then bound into small booklets which were bound together at the end of the year to make for the annual *Deputationsprotokoll*. This system created long and narrow pages; apparently the man charged with taking the minutes had a preference for that form -- it allowed enough space for a recording of the opinions (*vota*) and for a margin that contained various indications of the subjects under discussion. Once the small booklets had been prepared, the scribe had marked off a page as the space he would need to record one meeting. More often than not this arrangement proved to be too generous, since he only needed a half or two-thirds of that space. At the meetings he took down in pencil what interested him, and though he made no effort to copy all that was said, he did write with some haste: his handwriting may not have been as illegible as that of the Emperor but it did create real problems for anyone brave enough to decode it. Sometime after the meeting he went back over his original with pen and ink, so as to make the record a more permanent one. At this time he allowed himself the luxury of corrections, additions, and deletions, and the *protocollum* arrived at the state in which it would be found when *Faszikel 36* of the Vorträge was displayed to the learned and the merely curious.

The minutes of the meetings of the Deputation were still in rather rough form, and the same scribe would have to process what he had written to the point where it could be presented to the Emperor in the official form of a relation of the meeting. The relations tended to be longer and more verbose; they also removed a number of impurities that had been picked up during the preparation of the protocol -- gossip, the personal opinions of the scribe to the extent that they were unofficial, and anything that might serve to increase rather than decrease interdepartmental rivalries. These more elegant and ultimately less interesting documents did not have the good fortune to survive in any great number; they are often found in the collections of the War Council and the Treasury -- reminders of how interested some of the members of the Deputation had been in the official record of their efforts.[1] But the loss of the relations is more than made good by the preservation of the minutes in the rough and revealing state of the booklets, for much of the unique atmosphere of this committee would be lost if we could not consult this scribe at his chatty and often malicious best. The temptation to compress what happened at the meetings into a few conventional categories loses all of its power to reduce something that can be perceived in all of its historical individuality to the level of administrative convention.

As if to lend support to any enterprise that would take his minutes seriously the scribe made occasional use of a cipher. The hint of mystery that he managed to produce was not fated to be eternal, because he had the good sense to base his cipher on the Greek alphabet. He had obviously used it to prevent anyone reading over his shoulder from grasping the import of his moments of candor during the meetings. The language which he used was basically that of the *Ordnung und Instruction*; haste forced him to be ungrammatical at times and to use the subjunctive mood, when the indicative would have been more to the point. Frequently he lapsed into Latin, though this was not to be taken as a sign that the *votum* had been expressed in that language. For a secretary who had a decent command of the Latin language it often made good sense and saved time to translate the long and tortuous German sentences into their briefer Latin equivalents. In this way a few conventional phrases saved him the trouble of reproducing much that was baroque in its redundance. This shorthand through the means of translation made it difficult to determine how much he left out and what relation there was between the entries in his minutes and the actual length of the meetings. He acted, then, as both reporter and editor, seeking to represent the reality of those sessions as closely as he could and, at the same time, lingering on important points that were made, on the evolving line of the argument that eventually produced a conclusion. In performing these demanding tasks the scribe did more than convey the atmosphere of the Deputation; he managed to secure a place for himself in the small company of lively and well-informed observers and critics of Austrian administrative practice. Without being entirely aware of the fact this man wrote his history of the Deputation and insured that anyone else who would wish to do the same would be eternally in his debt. The very care he took in keeping the record, in writing that history, said more about the rise and fall of the Deputation than pages of learned commentary. As the initial high hopes began to dissipate and the miracle that had been expected did mot materialize carelessness began to creep into the *Deputationsprotokoll*; he spent less time in preparing the minutes, and his lists of absentee members revealed a sobering truth: the men on whom the Deputation depended for its viability had begun to turn away from it and to relapse into an official apathy that was more consistent with their pessimistic view of fundamental reform.

The extent to which this account of the Deputation depends on the work of its Secretary makes it natural to inquire as to his name and to the position he held in the administrative apparatus. The names of a number of *Referendare* who attended the meetings have been preserved -- Palm, Ilayren, Wöber -- and anyone of them might seem to qualify for the distinction of being the committee's Secretary. The individual who imposed his personality in so memorable a way on the minutes did not bother to identify himself or to give any strong indications as to his probable identity. On the basis of internal evidence the *Referendare* do not qualify; he referred to them in the third person and made it quite clear that at least one of them was keeping a protocol of his own. Attempts to discover him on the basis of his handwriting have been no more successful. If he wished to preserve his anonymity he can be complimented on the way it has defied the best efforts of acknowledged experts to find him out.[2]

The identity of the Secretary may not be as important as it would seem to be at a first glance. For even if we had his name we would probably have not much more to go on. The men who had such positions in the Austrian official hierarchy in the reign of Leopold I left few hints to serve a posterity that might interest itself in their lives and careers.[3] If they happened to be nobles they might hope for salvation from the genealogists or the family chroniclers, but if they were simply engaged in building a reputation or a bureaucratic dynasty the record was murky indeed. What was more to the point than the name was the position held by our Secretary, for this will have much to say about the point of view from which he wrote. But because he gives us no solid information on his exact location in the official machinery we have to sift what he says for precious clues as to his official identity. Thus if he supports one office against the competing officers it would be safe to conclude that he served in that office. His minutes, however, reveal a high degree of objectivity in the matter of offices; even though he seems to have sympathized with the military he did so not in the style of a *Referendar* (Wöber was there in any case) from the War Council but with the air of a man who did not like to see one man or one body blamed for all of the chaos and confusion.[4] The fact that he did not reveal any suspicious *partipris* is an indication that he stood above the battle of offices and agencies, that he was in fact one of the *Secretarii secreti* who worked closely with the Emperor. The Emperor had at his disposal a private chancellery (*Geheime Kanzlei*) that took care of his correspondence and often performed the absolutely necessary office of transliterating letters he had written in his own hand. These men were secretaries and without any evident rank or special favor, but it was in the very nature of their office that they had power and influence and did not feel at all hesitant about making their positions clear. They observed the workings of the Leopoldinian system from the best of all vantage points and managed somehow to maintain a fierce loyalty to the Emperor and a large measure of scepticism about the men and institutions that served him at lower levels. The government of Austria under Leopold was not a cabinet government, that is Leopold did not seek to dominate the system by issuing orders from his cabinet and depending on his secretaries to make sure that these orders were carried out. His *secretarii secreti* did not presume to possess that much power, but, as in the case of our Secretary, they could be wonderfully useful in observing the workings of the Imperial *collegia* and committees. The Secretary of the Deputation could be expected, then, to do more than keep the record straight; he could make it possible for the Emperor to be in constant touch with the proceedings by keeping minutes that were not simply passive responses to a situation but the passionate and involved participation of a man who felt that he had a great stake in a successful outcome.[5]

The Secretary had presumably been assigned to the Deputation at the request of Kinsky. Since the committee did not have a permanent staff or its own records it would be necessary to secure help from an already existing agency and what made for a better arrangement than a loan of a secretary from the Privy Chancellery. The Chairman would make his own reports to the Emperor, but they could not be considered substitutes for a detailed account of each meeting. For that particular service the Secretary would be most useful. And so the Secretary joined the Deputation and assisted the Chairman without becoming the Chairman's man; his first loyalty was to the Emperor, and it was this commitment that would make it possible for him to reveal even Count Kinsky, among others, in a not wholly favorable light. For while the Emperor trusted Kinsky and regarded him as the minister most capable of leading the Deputation he still wanted to have some idea as to how Kinsky was behaving himself and whether or not the minister's justly famous ability to arouse antipathy in other people had become an obstacle to the creation of a consensus in the committee.[6] Kinsky might have been distressed if he had realized just how graphic a picture the Secretary was presenting for Leopold's edification, but he could hardly complain about the practice, since he had been known to make use of apparently harmless secretaries to further his own political designs.[7] The other members had even more reason to complain about the partisan views expressed by the Secretary, but if they knew of their existence they gave no sign. His presence at the meetings did not prevent them from expressing themselves with a good deal of candor and an occasional lack of moderation.

The Secretary acted as the recording angel for the Deputation, and he also was called upon to express his own opinions on matters under discussion. In the pecking order that operated in the committee he spoke after the chief officers of the various agencies and just before *Referendar* Palm, and though seniority may have been at work here this was a sign of the influence he possessed as a member of the Emperor's private staff. His opinions were usually noted down simply as *"meum votum"* with that rubric occasionally in his cipher.[8] The statement of the opinion that followed could at times be fairly detailed; it was difficult to resist the temptation to give himself sufficient coverage -- after all he had good reason to know how close he came to expressing a truly adequate statement of the government's position. He might complain that Cout Max Ludwig Breuner was more than a little prolix (*"satis fusum"*), but his main complaint against the General War Commissar was his patent refusal to learn anything, to extend his mental horizons beyond their very obvious limits.[9] On occasion he also felt moved to complain about a complete misreading of a situation, but a reaction of this kind could not be expressed in public and had to be reserved for the minutes.[10]

In the discussions of the new repartition in Hungary he pursued a most sophisticated line. He was realist enough to expect that the money would not be obtained, that the tough line espoused by the Hungarian leaders probably rested on a solid basis of fact. No one could be certain that the government would be able to overcome Hungarian resistance. "Meanwhile a great insurrection is to be feared."[11] When he was going over this statement, he made an additional remark just after the reference to insurrection: "Still, it must be tried." He and some of his fellow members of the Deputation realized how much risk there was in the new system of *contributio* and were not at all optimistic about the outcome, but in the face of approaching financial doom the government could not afford to accept without question the Hungarian assurances that the additional two million gulden could not be raised in Hungary.

On another occasion the Secretary revealed a similar nuanced awareness of the factors governing Hungarian resistance. He declared that it was too much to expect to demand that the nobility and clergy assume one-third of the total sum. Archbishop Széchényi reported an income of eight hundred gulden and was required by the new system to pay forty thousand. On the other hand, the nobility and clergy would have to do better than one-thirtieth of the total -- "...to jump from a third to a thirtieth was to jump too far." Then no one would ever pay the tax. "Our sacred intention is to relieve the burden on the *misera plebs* and the cities but the business must be handled in such a way that we will have some measure of success." He finally came down in favor of a compromise: the nobility and clergy should pay as much as the cities (one-sixteenth). This *votum* expressed the growing feeling in official circles that a compromise was necessary; the pious hopes of the Emperor had to yield to political realities. If the nobility in Hungary was pressed too far the logical consequence would be a revolt against the Habsburgs that would be far more dangerous than the peasant uprising led by Ferenc Tokaji.[12]

The Secretary did not always confine himself to an expression of the various options that had to be taken into consideration before a final decision could be made. There were moments when he came down firmly on the side of dramatic action, as when he discussed the policy of the government in reference to military excesses in Hungary:

> I consider it absolutely necessary to make an example in this case. These excesses and brutalities have received a good deal of attention; they destroy all love for the Emperor. (The gentlemen who perpetrated these deeds) don't seem to realize that majesty and power are firmly rooted in the affections of subjects (*...quod maiestas et potentia consistat in affecta subditorum*).[13]

No one will ever be able to determine the extent to which the Secretary expressed the views of the professional bureaucrats in the Austrian administration, but there is no reason to believe that he differed in any important way from the general position of his colleagues, the Palms, the Mayrens, the Wöbers who kept the notoriously creaky machinery in some passable state of repair. These men rejoiced in an education that far exceeded that of many of their superiors. They had a more than passing acquaintance with hard and monotonous work. When it came to expressing their views of policy they were not clearly mindless advocates of more advanced and centralized government. Money was desperately needed -- they knew that better than anyone else -- but this did not impel them to make a radical break with the system within which they worked. The minutes that were kept by the *Secretarius secretus* provide a sure guide to the workings of the Deputation, but they do more than that. They reveal a mentality at work, a mentality that was drawn to innovation out of desperation rather than conviction and which, if it encountered much resistance, retired into compromise or even apathy. Hidden away in the most hopeful of these men was the gnawing fear that whatever they tried to do to relieve the situation it simply would not produce any results: "As I have often said, we won't get the money."[14]

Notes

1. The *Grosse Korrespondenz*, April 6, 1698, fol. 972-973, contains relations of the Deputation with the Emperor's resolution. There is a similar relation for the meeting of March 14, 1698 in the *Hofkammerarchiv: Hoffinanz, Ungarn*, Fasz. 387, fol. 67-73.

2. I am particularly grateful for the assistance of Prof. Walter Leitsch of the University of Vienna and Dr. Walter Pillich of the *Haus-, Hof- und Staatsarchiv* in the effort to establish the Secretary's identity. Though the case cannot be considered closed for good there is only a slight hope that the mystery will be eventually solved.

3. Max Braubach has noted this phenomenon which he encountered in seeking information on Palm: "Die genauen Lebensdaten von Palm waren nicht zu ermitteln.", *Prinz Eu von Savoyen: Eine Biographie* (Wien, 1963), I, 442.

4. "Onmia *contra militiam* quae *non fuerunt* ad rem.", *Deputationsprotokoll 1700*, Oct. 8, 1700, fol. 142-145; (words in cipher underlined).

5. That men like the Secretary were not without influence is demonstrated by the role of Palm and Locher in the sweeping changes in the government in 1703, cf. Braubach, *op. cit.*, I, 354, 366-367.

6. Leopold had a pronounced preference for availing himself of the services of men who were not of ministerial rank; indeed, he seemed to enjoy keeping some of them in the dark about utters of real importance, *ibid.*, I, 354.

7. In order to ensure that England's Mediator, Sir William Hussey, would not exceed the limits of his mediatorial function Kinsky introduced Count Marsigli into Hussey's official family as the ambassador's "secretary".
8.   As,for example, the notation: "Votum *meum* (underlined word in cipher), *Deputationsprotokoll 1698*, Sept. 22, 1698, fol. 217-218. On other occasions, he did not actually indicate that he was recording his own opinion; the belief that it was his is based on its place in the order of business and the fact that it is quite detailed, cf. *ibid.*, Oct. 20, 1698, fol. 230-232.

9. Breuner's verbosity was noted on June 30, 1699 in cipher, *Deputationsprotokoll 1699*, fol. 34; "Dominus Comes Breuner nihil *wult scire*." (underlined words in cipher), *ibid.*, Nov. 19, 1699, fol. 65.

10. At the end of a conclusion given by Kinsky the Secretary added: "Non est *ita*"(underlined word in cipher), *Deputationsprotokoll 1698*, "Sessio 75" (exact date not given, though it must have been at the end of August, 1698), fol. 204-210.

11. "Allegant autem impossibilitatem; an haec possit superari, me latet. Interesa timendi ugni motus. Tentandum tamen.", *ibid*, May 9, 1698, fol. 153-155.

12. "Offerunt 30. partem oder 3 pro cento von ihren proventibus,
Tertiam dare non possunt. Archiepiscopus dicit se habere 800 fl. und Bolle 40.000 fl.
geben.... A tertia saltant ad 30.; ist zu weith. Nihil unquam contribuerunt. Sie bey gutem
willen zu erhalten, mögte man ihnen wenigst so viehl zuemuthen, als die stett geben.",
ibid., Nov. 14, 1698, fol. 244-246.

13. *Deputationsprotokoll 1700*, Sept. 16, 1700, fol. 185-187.

14. "...sicut ego *dixi*, man verde es nicht haben." (underlined word in cipher),
Deputationsprotokoll 1699, May 25, 1699, fol. 29.

Chapter Six
In Rebus Hungaricis / Hungarian Dilemma

In its first official meetings which took place in December 1697 and January 1698 the Deputation found itself immediately confronted by the question of what was to be done with Hungary. All of its members had good reason to be familiar with the most recent negotiations with the Hungarians, and a few of them, faced with much the same problem as they had in the past, must have experienced a particularly lively sense of *déjà vu*. For some ten years before the Emperor had felt it necessary to make major decisions about Hungary's future, and he had asked his chief advisers to prepare a set of general recommendations. A new Court Commission (*Hofcommission*) had been called into being, and it had been peopled with members of the Privy Conference: Dietrichstein, Stratmann, Ernst Rüdiger Starhemberg, Orsini-Rosenberg, Kinsky, and Kollonich. Since many of these ministers felt that they had more pressing business elsewhere, a subcommittee had been required, and in this slightly less prestigious group Kollonich had presided. This committee was made up of representatives of offices that had an interest in a Hungarian settlement -- The Treasury, the Court Chancellery, the Bohemian Chancellery, and the War Council -- and among its members were Seyfried Breuner, Vice President of the Treasury at the time, and Julius Bucceleni, Austrian Vice Chancellor.[1]

In the months that followed, this subcommittee had done a

surprising amount of work for Austrian officials; after some eighty meetings they presented their recommendations in the form of a lengthy treatise that bore the iupressive title of *Hauptrelation Über die Einrichtung des Königreichs Hungarn.* The treatise was so long that it was accompanied by a conpendium for the use of busy officials, and the name was so unwieldy that it came to be called the *Einrichtungswerk.*[2]

Though Kollonich had been assisted by the members of the subcommittee, he soon came to be regarded as the one man most responsible for the nature of the recommendations that were made. In making his own views the generally accepted position of the subcommittee he deserved some fame as the Monarchy's chief authority on Hungary and as the author of a most substantial contribution to the literature of Habsburg planning for the future of Hungary.[3] His *Einrichtungswerk* did not contain anything that might be described as general axioms to govern Austrian policy in years to come; it hugged the more mundane path of administrative reform that had some bearing on legal and ecclesiastical questions as well. It did lean precariously in the direction of a Catholic centralization for the Habsburg dominions, Hungary included, and this natural tendency of the times was supported by arguments derived from theories of Natural Law and from the more impressive suggestions of the Austrian cameralists.

Yet for all its patina of modernity, the plan assumed the peaceful co-existence of a strong central government and Hungarian constitutioflalism -- once the more outstanding sources of disagreement had been removed. Hungary, whose constitutional and social organization remained more traditional than that of the neighboring Austrian and Bohemian lands, was to be admitted to the Habsburg 'family of nations' without first undergoing any radical modifications in its political and social forms, though it was equally clear from the recommendations that any thoroughgoing effort by the Hungarians to preserve the Ständestaat in its fullness would have to be abandoned. This was particularly true in the matter of the nobles' claim of freedom from taxation. Since they were no longer required to join their

Apostolic (and hereditary) King with their feudal retinues in time of war, Kollonich believed that they should contribute to the cost of the maintenance of Habsburg administration of Hungary and thus assume a respectable proportion of the costs of the Imperial military machine. There was nothing excessively Germanizing or anti-Hungarian in such a suggestion, but it ran head on into the most treasured privilege of the Hungarian ruling classes and in so doing suggested that the future Primate of Hungary had not grasped the exact nature of the struggle between the Vienna government and the Hungarians.

The balance of the recommendations considered means of modernizing Hungarian judicial, financial, and ecclesiastical institutions. Judges were to be made independent of the royal administration (this was a very progressive recommendation), and a greater equality before the law was to be established for all classes of Hungarians. Kollonich set a limit to the amount of time the peasants were to work the lands of their lords, and even though the limit was a modest one it did point to a growing awareness of the need for inproving the condition of the peasantry.[4]   Kollonich's special interest, the status of the Catholic Church in the Kingdom of St. Stephen, led him to suggest a general tightening up of parochial and diocesan organization which had become most lax and confused during the long period of Turkish occupation.

For all its obvious omissions and its cavalier manner of dealing with real points at issue between the central government and the reumants of the *Ständestaat*, the *Einrichtungswerk* constituted a thoughtful set of proposals by a man full of good intentions and administrative experience. The nature of his political education had been such as to limit his view of the whole Hungarian horizon to questions of administrative practice and of readjustments of financial responsibilities. It was difficult to see how the suggestion could be made that these recommendations were to be taken as proof of the high degree of culture in social, political, and economic affairs possessed by Leopold I's ministers.[5]   The absence, rather than the presence of any pronounced current of political theorizing at his Court is only further underlined by such a document.   The misfortune here may have been that even these proposals were condemned to remain proposals, that relatively little was done to carry them into practice. But a sign had been given of a will to carry through change in Hungary and to begin with the taxation of the nobility and measures calculated to remove some of the misery from the term *misera plebs contribuens*.

The situation had undergone relatively little change, when the Deputation met on February 14, 1698. Though it had a clear mandate to act decisively in regard to Hungary, the discussion continued to center around the all too familiar questions of *quantum*? and *guale*? The *fundus* that had been set at a figure of twelve million gulden continued to play its magical role in the deliberations, though there were signs even at this early stage that this figure rested ultimately on optimism and not on a realistic assessment of the situation. Time alone seemed to be in short supply, and the opinion was expressed that the twelve million gulden might indeed be raised but only long after the financial crisis had descended upon the Austrian government. Still, the pressing character of their obligation, as members of the Deputation, to assist the Emperor in averting such a disaster did not prevent them from indulging in the fine old Viennese custom of prolonged and occasionally irrelevant discussion. Kinsky sounded so true to character in expressing the opinion -- it stood as a sort of conclusion to the deliberations -- that they must proceed with great care and arrive at a decision only after canvassing all of the possibilities.[6]

In the course of this preliminary discussion three specific proposals were made that had to do with Hungary: first, that the clergy, the magnates, and the nobles, the cities and the peasants were to receive fair treatment, based on their ability to pay; second, that the excise tax system then in operation in the Hereditary Lands should be introduced into Hungary; third, that the repartition was to be prepared as quickly as possible so that it could be forwarded to Bratislava and then to the *comitats* with a date set for the expiration of the payments. A further suggestion was made that the presence in Bratislava of Cardinal Kollonich would be of great assistance in expediting these procedures.[7] It was inportant to be expeditious in this affair because the rigors of winter were already depleting the ranks of the taxpayers in Hungary -- a goodly number were reported to be seeking refuge from the inclement weather and the persistent tax collectors in the more relaxed atmosphere of the Ottoman Enpire. The Deputation noted in passing that the Hungarians were not the only problem children: the Austrians had been showing increasing reluctance to pay their taxes in full. Even the grudging votes of supply (*Bewilligungen*) of the Austrian Diets had not spurred the taxpaers to any great exertions.[8]

On February 20, 1698, the Deputation returned to the knotty question of the most efficient system of direct and indirect taxes for Hungary. Kollonich expressed his reservations about the value of his trip to Bratislava; he felt that it was pointless to enter into discussions with leading Hungarian officials and then to wait expectantly for the money. Only when the gulden were flowing into the Treasury would it be time to do the talking. Yet he expressed his first doubts about the size of Hungary's share of the total *contributio*. Since there appeared to be no sign of any readiness to compromise on the figure of four million gulden, however, he had a suggestion to make that might help to solve the problem of *quale*? The peasants and the cities should pay half of that -- two million gulden -- and the clergy, the magnates, and the gentry assume responsibility for the remainder. The Deputation raised no objections to what he had said, but the members were most interested in seeing that the Primate assume personal charge of the Hungarian repartition. They were obviously afraid that if that was left to the mercies of the Hungarian administration the privileged classes would evade their unquestioned responsibility by siuply not paying their portion of the amount. Kollonich had no illusions about the response his programme was likely to receive. He could foresee a need for military assistance to encourage and even coupel payment, if all official pleas met with no success. It would require a small army of officials from the Treasury and the General War Commissariat to make certain that all segments of Hungarian society paid their share.[9]

When word of this new policy reached Bratislava, the Palatine responded with a forceful appeal to the Deputation. The reports that he had received of the latest plans for the Hungarian repartition were not calculated to ease an already tense situation. For once he did not indulge his taste for wide-ranging *gravamina* but addressed himself directly to the proposed repartition. And in so doing he registered a strong protest against the radical innovation of requiring the privileged orders to pay the tax. His protest had little immediate effect, and the Deputation continued to be adamant in its view that any resistance to its recent directives would be inconsistent with loyalty to the Emperor who had after all given his august approval to the new plan. Once again, the view was expressed that all Hungarians were to share the burden. Special care had to be taken to make certain that the "weight of the tax load was not transferred to the weaker by the stronger." The Palatine and his associates were given the chill comfort of a promise of a visit from Cardinal Kollonich. In the meantime the Deputation expected that the Palatine would carry out the repartition along lines that had been established by the committee.[10]

The long-awaited visit of the Cardinal did finally take place, but his presence was not sufficient in itself to overawe the reluctant Hungarians. Early in May, the Deputation received a personal visit from the Palatine, and the exceedingly delicate matter of the "remaining two millions" (this was a sign that the Hungarians were ready to pay two million gulden and believed that anything in addition was excessive) came into the official discussion once more. Prince Esterházy spoke in his official capacity as the Palatine, but he also could be regarded now as the spokesman for the Hungarian magnates who lived in Vienna and for a number of others who had been moved to visit the capital on learning of the new tax policy. He wisely restricted himself to a discussion of the technical problems arising out of the Deputation's decision, but he made no secret of his desire to secure some concessions for the Hungarian nobility. A move in this direction could be noted in his request for permission to call a conference of delegates from the *comitats* that would meet and discuss the whole question at Vienna.[11]

While the Palatine sounded out the members of the Deputation, Kollonich met with the Hungarian leaders then meeting in Vienna. With the greatest show of reluctance they conceded him the point of the four million gulden and even went to the length of expressing a willingness to have that sum collected, if need be, by the extreme measure of execution, a brutally confiscatory device carried out by the military. But one of these magnates had sufficient courage to warn the Cardinal that this policy would most certainly lead to a general rebellion in Hungary. But this did not disturb His Eminence's serenity of spirit; he continued to discount any talk of the danger of rebellion.[12]

The very next session of the Deputation devoted itself to a careful consideration of a formal statement that had been submitted by the Hungarians. There were signs of growing pessimism about the likelihood of collecting the additional two million gulden even if some face-saving agreement was reached with the Hungarians. The Secretary brought his characteristic frankness to the discussion: "The Treasury will never set its eyes on the sum in question." He still believed that the Hungarians had the capability of paying despite their denials that they could. Of one thing he was certain and that was that in forcing through its programme the Austrian government made insurrection virtually inevitable.[13] The iron law of Hungarian politics had not escaped his discerning mind: any increase in the financial strain inposed upon Hungary would be reflected in a proportional increment in the danger of revolt. The task facing the Deputation was not unlike that of the physician testing for degrees of pain; what it had to avoid at all costs was reaching that point of no return where a Hungary *in tormentis* went over to open revolt against Austrian rule. But the relentless nature of the Emperor's financial obligations made it virtually impossible for his ministers to be overly squeamish about crossing Hungary's pain threshold.

At this particular point in the discussion opinions could differ on the degree of danger of an insurrection: Kollonich was still calm, while the Secretary made no secret of his apprehensions. The reply that was officially made by the Emperor to the memorial of the Hungarians gave no hint of concern. Leopold seemed to be in no mood to quibble with the Hungarians, and it was with the greatest show of an irrevocable decision that he declared that he could not possibly reduce his demand for the full sum of four million gulden. His statement was not without its unconscious irony: "His Sacred Majesty accepts with a grateful heart the undertaking of the lords, the Primate, the Palatine, and the magnates to raise the full sum in the space of twelve months." [14]   But this did not prevent the Palatine from continuing to hope that even this final expression of the Imperial will did not close the door on further negotiation even though he was privately assured that this was indeed Leopold's "last word". [15]

The Deputation reached the next stage in this complex and bitter dispute in June of that year, when the Palatine submitted yet another memorial that took up the question of the repartition. He now appeared to be accepting the Deputation's programme as a *fait accompli*, but no one could doubt that the Hungarian administrative apparatus, particularly at the local level, would be used to place obstacles in the way of any token policy of fulfillment. Kollonich, as if to avoid such a fate for his programme and that of the Deputation, asked that the records of the *comitat* tax recorders be sent on to Vienna, so that it might be possible in working out the repartition to have all the necessary facts at hand. But it was objected that it would consume too long a period of time to bring these records to Vienna; this would only slow down the final promulgation of the repartition. Time was so pressing that it became increasingly clear that the Deputation would have to accept the Palatine's assurances and the form of repartition which he proposed. [16]

As if to confess a need for diversion, the Deputation now turned its attention to the situation in the Hereditary Lands, where there were quite as many problems and opinions of what should be done. Now members of the Deputation who had close working ties with the various lands began to complain that the programme did not provide for preferential treatment of any of the Hereditary lands. In the course of the debate on this point ministerial tempers, which had been under a great strain during the negotiations with the Hungarians, now began to reveal themselves in no uncertain way. The indecisive Kinsky found himself in the uncongenial role of urging the members to abide by its previous determination to insure equal treatment of the lands and provinces; he felt that it would be a dangerous precedent to reopen debate time and time again on questions which had been regarded as decided for once and for all. In his two capacities of Chairman and Supreme Bohemian Chancellor he urged his colleagues to adhere to the policies they had already laid down. A spirited interchange with Count Bucceleni developed, and the Chairman so far forgot himself as to observe that the Buccelenis had always been a troublesome lot.[17]

This contretemps may well have cleared the atmosphere, and Kinsky went on with the business of stating the conclusions of the session as if nothing had happened. He reiterated the belief that the Deputation had a stake in treating the Hereditary Lands on terms of equality. This position, once established, must be maintained as a standing practice. Any chances in the *fundus* or exceptions to this general rule would cause irreparable harm and lead to a further deterioration of the government's financial situation, the very thing the Deputation had been called into being to prevent. But Kinsky would not have been Kinsky if he had not relented at the very end of his *conclusum*: no change would be tolerated in the amount that had been levied on each land but within that basic framework concessions to local conditions might be permitted.[18] Rigid equality and a respect for local variations made for strange partners indeed. As Kinsky envisioned it, a mystical harmony could and must be established between the Emperor's duty to treat all of his subjects as equals and his equally sacred responsibility to respect local privileges.

Leopold approved Kinsky's conclusion in a subsequent resolution, but he refrained, perhaps wisely, from repeating his minister's finer points of argumentation. As the father of his peoples, Leopold could not permit any inequality to exist, especially in so grave a time as this. He was prepared to follow local practice in collecting the taxes so long as the sum he required could be obtained. Kinsky had reported to him that the Deputation anticipated that the Hungarians would go ahead with their own repatition. "No one shall be exempted, but the manner of collection may be left to the *comitats*." [19] Apparently the Emperor wished to bring Hungary into line with the rest of his dominions; it was a move that was eminently reasonable from his point of view but it would not fail to evoke the most stubborn of opposition in Hungary.

By the end of June 1698, the Deputation had still not settled the repartition for Hungary. Indeed, it found itself considering the Palatine's suggestion that delegates of the *comitats* be summoned to

Vienna to discuss the entire tax situation with the Imperial ministers. Again, Cardinal Kollonich opposed such a plan as being to little purpose: it would be costly and chaotic -- each *comitat* had its own system of tax collection. But Kinsky reported to the Deputation that the Emperor had agreed to allow the delegates to come to Vienna; this step would fit in with his practice of summoning the chief officials of the lands to Vienna for exploratory talks on the amounts they would be expected to secure from their Diets. Now that Leopold's decision had been made, Kinsky indicated that there must be an end to further discussion.[20] Silence reigned for once and extended its sway over the planning for the next round with the Hungarians. This may well have been a sign of diminished energies and resolution; the Deputation was already beginning to show evident signs of mental and emotional fatigue.

During the summer of 1698 the talk shifted to other aspects of the great overall problem of finances. Now it was Transylvania's turn to move to the foreground, and no one could deny that the situation there already approached the status of a general crisis.[21] But September brought with it the reappearance of Prince Esterházy. He had arrived in Vienna to oversee the preparations for the conference of delegates, and the statement he made to the Deputation on September 18, had been composed under the impact of conversations he had been having with the first wave of Hungarian delegates. These gentlemen had had an adverse effect on the Palatine, for they had encouraged the quite malleable spokesman for their cause to adopt a more intransigent position: he now argued that in accord with the ancient laws of Hungary that had been duly recognized by its Habsburg kings matters of a purely Hungarian nature could not be decided upon outside Hungary. This meant that the question of the war-tax must be referred to the Hungarian administration in Bratislava and, what was more to the point, to a Hungarian Diet. The Palatine was still reluctant to mention the calling of the Diet, but it was clearly very much in his mind and in the minds of the Hungarian magnates and gentry.

The Deputation found itself to be quite unmoved by the Palatine's insistence on the antiquity of the laws that forbade discussion outside of Hungary. Much had happened in the past one hundred and fifty years to modify the conditions that had produced such legislation. Moreover, the Hungarians had shown little interest themselves in these particular laws. They had requested the conference at Vienna, and for the past two years had been submitting proposals to the government that contained no reference to the illegality of any decision the ministers might make. The mood of the Deputation was not a propitious one for a successful outcome of these talks. Its replies to Hungarian arguments were makeshift and barren of any sincere effort to preserve equality and individuality -- all at one and the same time. But even the aristocrats who dominated the committee and its meetings had begun to see that the explanation for the most recent Hungarian demands was to be situated in the selfish attitude of Hungary's upper classes. They simply did not wish to pay the tax and used the pious talk of ancient privileges as a smokescreen. If the whole question was to be referred to Bratislava the stronger segments of Hungarian society would indeed triumph over the weaker ones.[22]

The none too oblique threat of a Hungarian Diet produced a united front in the Deputation. For once the members were in complete agreement: there was to be no Diet at this time. If Kinsky in drawing the usual conclusions from the discussion adopted a more moderate tone he probably did so in the expectation that what he said would be used as the basis for the Emperor's answer to the Hungarians. The most likely way out of the impasse, according to him, was to assure them that the new tax programme bypassed the usual Hungarian official channels and class interests only out of sheer necessity.[23] This theme did reappear in the Imperial resolution in which Leopold declared that he had no intention of assailing the privileges of the Hungarian Estates. No one could be more interested than he in seeing the Kingdom of St. Stephen restored to the full possession of its laws and customs. *"Salus populi suprema lex"*; the expression seemed out of place in this discussion, but there was good reason to believe that it expressed one theme in Leopold's variegated thinking about his official role.

He went on to remind the Hungarians of some recent history: the desperate state of his finances and the summoning of the *comitat* representatives to Vienna. His conduct had contained no illegality or offense to the Hungarian constitution; he had only availed himself of the format of the *Concurszus*, which had been tried so often in past years. The Emperor's argumentation had indeed been patterned on Kinsky' s *conclusum*; the sense of emergency which it conveyed had given additional coherence and vigor to Leopold's point of view. He now confidently expected that his "*deputirte ministerium*" would put an end to the present imbroglio by coming to a working agreement with the Hungarians. If it failed to achieve what he wanted by discussion and negotiation the Emperor might find himself forced to make other arrangements.[24]

Additional discussion added nothing new to what had become conventional features of the interchanges. The constant flow of grievances from the Hungarian side encountered quite as steady a flow of orders and admonitions from the Deputation. The committee held fast to its decision that there were to be no exceptions from the obligation to pay the tax; it seemed a relatively simple matter to have all and sundry contribute "according to their means." The Hungarians were informed that their convocation would not be adjourned until a settlement had been reached on the repartition that was in accord with the expressed wish of the Emperor. Imperial patience continued to be in short supply, and the Emperor was almost peevish as he continued to press for the final agreement.[25]

Weeks passed without any sign of change in the two immobile positions; the best that could be said of the arrnagement was that the subject was still under consideration. On October 20, Kollonich told the Deputation that Archbishop Szechenyi had been to visit him the previous day and, speaking in the name of all the Hungarians meeting in Vienna, had declared that they were unable to give their assent to the demands of the Emperor without securing the official sanction of the Hungarian Diet. But this was not to be the only piece of bad news that day; reports had reached old Starhemberg that a peasant uprising in the vicinity of Munkacs was aimed not so much at the Habsburg military formations in the area but at the Hungarian landowning class.[27] There could be no more pointed comment by the *misera plebs* on the negotiations in Vienna, but the news gave little aid or comfort to the

Austrian ministers. They regarded it as yet another good reason for reaching some kind of agzwement with the Hungarian convocation.

By now the condition of the regiments in Hungary had become desperate. The long arrears in pay and the lack of supplies made it doubtful how long these units could be depended upon as organized bodies of soldiers. One member of the Deputation now suggested that a repartition for Hungary should be drawn up in Vienna (he refused to go into the vexed question of the legality of such a move) and submitted as soon as possible to the inspection of the three most interested parties: the Treasury, the War Council, the War Commissariat. Soon the army would have to take up winter quarters, and this meant that the officials of all these offices would have to have some idea of what funds they could expect from the Hungarians.[28]

The Hungarians had their own version of the repartition, but it was Palm's opinion that it was quite unacceptable. Perhaps it might help, however, to use it for purposes of comparison with another version that had been tentatively prepared with an eye to just such an emergency by the War Commissariat. Palm's attitude must have been characteristic of the rest of the committee, for there was a general feeling that the whole responsibility for the continued state of indecision rested with the Hungarians. The suspicion was growing that the Hungarians had not been acting in good faith but had been making use of a wide variety of delaying tactics. So sweeping a condemnation of the 'adversary' failed to be entirely convincing, but it was an index of the frustration felt by those who had the awesome assignment of bringing the Hungarians around to an acceptance of certain political and financial realities. But at the very moment that the Deputation reached the most unyielding posture in this long discussion the first hint of approaching compromise appeared. Without any long preparation or evidence of thought the committee now declared that the peasants would have to be responsible for two-thirds of the tax, the upper classes the remaining third. Kollonich, who had been in constant communication with the Hungarian delegates in the utterly thankless role of go-between, was instructed to convey this latest calculation to them. The Deputation believed that the magnates would take immediate steps to revise their draft of the repartition on this new ratio.[29]

A week later, this directive was amplified to include the Hungarian cities: they were to contribute one-sixteenth of the total. Count Kaunitz, once the initial break had come in the discussions, came forward as an exponent of a policy of moderation vis-a-vis Hungary's privileged classes -- he had no wish to see the nobility and the clergy pressed too far. Let there be repeated assurances given to them that the present plan was only valid for one year; it was an emergency measure and not a permanent arrangement.[30] His colleagues agreed with him that everything that could be done to quiet the fears expressed by the Hungarians should be tried out. This may have opened the way to a new inspiration: "...the present system will remain in force until they (i.e. the Hungarians) suggest a more suitable one." Austrian officials tiring of the chase began to be less careful in formulating their opinions. They had come to realize at long last that the Hungarians would do everything in their power (and it was not to be easily discounted) to preserve the status quo; they would find the means to escape from what they felt to be an intolerable exaction. In this way injustice would breed more injustice, as force was required to carry out the present system. All that the ministers could do at such a juncture was to echo the pious hope that a close watch would be kept on the *comitats* during the time of actual tax collection.[31]

The men of the Deputation might be excused for feeling that they had said the last word on the subject, and that word was 'force'. But this confidence was to be short-lived. On November 12, the Palatine returned to the attack with a new statement that indicated how little actual progress had been made. Esterházy had his turn at being disingenuous: he "understood that a third of the contribution was to be paid by the clergy and the nobility, and he could only hope that it was not the intention of His Majesty that the Hungarian nobility perish." This led him immediately into a graphic picture of conditions in Hungary. Barely eight of the fifty-two *comitats* were in what might be called a normal state; the flight of taxpayers to a haven in the Ottoman Empire continued; the nobility faced ruin that would be quite as complete as that menacing the common people. He reminded the Deputation that

Hungary had chosen a Habsburg as its king of its own free will; it had no reason to expect treatment of the kind that it was receiving now. He then requested that a totally different system of taxation be established -- "it would be an easy matter to discover one" -- and suggested that a special commission be formed to study the whole question.[32]

It was not surprising that the Deputation reacted strongly to what might be considered a frontal attack on its prerogatives, but what was surprising was the new tolerance its members displayed in discussing the latest Hungarian move. Perhaps too long a confrontation with the abyss that was the Hungarian question had left them wiser and more chastened men. Up to now it had dealt with the Palatine in writing to a large degree. In the new mood of sweet reasonableness it declared that it was ready to receive the Palatine in person the very next day.[33]

Esterházy appeared at the appointed time, supported by Archbishop Széchényi, the Hungarian Chancellor, and two of his assistants. Kinsky told them at the very outset that they owed their day in court to the gracious desire of the Emperor that the Hungarians be heard once more. In the meantime, they were given to understand that all the previous directives of the Deputation remained in force.[34] Whether or not the Hungarians felt any gratitude was hard to tell, for they went about the usual business of airing their grievances with the same tiresome insistence. One point they did make with the greatest solemnity and that was their allegation that the clergy and the nobility could not pay one-third of the *contributio*. Arbhbishop Széchényi sought to drive this point home by making reference to his own predicament: he received eight hundred gulden in income and yet he was required by the present amended system to pay forty thousand in taxes. This inequity was repeated in innumerable instances: the peasants, for example, had to pay the Treasury three times the taxes they had paid the Turks, and they were expected to furnish the soldiers with food and quarters as well. Then the Archbishop took another tack, and one that might be dangerous in the long run for his side, since it rested upon a comparison of the Hungarian situation and that prevailing in the Hereditary Lands. But he could not resist a sly thrust at the Austrian and Bohemian magnates who expected their opposite numbers in Hungary to pay one-third by reminding them that the clergy and the nobility of the Hereditary Lands had never been required to pay that much. At this telling point, the discussion concluded for the day, and the Hungarians were told to return on the morrow for further talks.[35]

In the interim the Palatine probably felt that the Deputation had shown signs of weakening -- the reference to the tax quotas in the Hereditary Lands had had its effect by now -- and so he returned to the committee meeting with every sign of carrying the day for the Hungarian view. He reminded Kollonich that the Hungarians had always prepared their own repartition; they felt this to be their right. According to the customs of their country, they must retain this power in their hands. Once he had made that initial point, he was ready to be specific in discussing the breakdown of the repartition. The royal cities were ready now to pay one-sixteenth of the four million total, and they had the support of the clergy and the nobility in this. But then the Palatine unwrapped the surprise package of the day before the horrified eyes of the members of the Deputation: the nobility now declared itself ready to contribute one-thirtieth of the tax, that is the magnificent sum of 133,333 gulden.[36] On the strength of that revelation the Hungarians were asked to withdraw, while the Deputation considered what its next step would be.

It could be certain of a quarter of a million gulden from the cities and an additional 133,333 gulden from the three upper orders of Hungary. That still left 3,616,667 gulden (in the excitement of the moment some hasty computations produced an incorrect sum of 3,061,666 gulden), and it was painfully evident that it would have to come from one and only one source -- the peasantry.[37] The committee pretended to find it convenient to confine the discussion to facts and figures without referring to previously held positions, and this new pragmatic mood strengthened the hand of the people who were interested in making concessions to the Hungarians. Kaunitz, for example, gave out the opinion that the demand for one-third would never work, but he was not ready as yet to give his assent to one-thirtieth or three per cent. It seemed to him that twice the amount to be contributed by the cities was reasonable, that is one-eighth or half a million gulden. And this was the sum that the Deputation found to be to its taste, though in grasping for this straw no one could display much enthusiasm or certainty that that would be the end of the discussion.[38]

It was not the final word in fact, for on November 17, 1698, the Hungarians gave notice that the only way out of the present impasse was to settle on the figure of one-twenty-fourth or 166,666 gulden.[39] This bargaining back and forth continued down to the very end of the year, and it was ended only when the Emperor intervened with another show of decision and established the sum of 250,000 gulden (one-sixteenth) as the final figure. The Deputation might wonder how "*der arme mann*" would ever be able to produce three and a half million gulden, but as a slave to its conscience it promised that a measure of relief would be given to the common people by reducing the levies on food for the soldiers quartered in Hungary.[40]

The first weeks of 1699 were devoted to a consideration of the problems arising out of the implementation of the repartition now that one had finally been agreed upon after so many months of negotiation. The most flagrant abuses were reported in the *comitats*; the money was not arriving with the speed and in the abundance that had been expected, and even this most inequitable of tax programmes became more unjust at the local level. The Deputation's agendas became clogged with endless complaints about these practices. Surprise, indignation, and then frustration, the whole armory of emotions available to a harried and virtually powerless official committee, were increasingly evident. The Deputation loyally recommended that each and every case be investigated and that wherever it seemed justified in individual cases exceptions were to be made. But on the *fundus* itself and the basic, though much sabotaged, principle of the taxation of all classes in Hungary no concession could be made.[41] After a year of activity the Deputation was still unwilling to advise the Emperor to carry through his new programme with the use of force, and there was the consequent growth of an interest in seeing what the Palatine and his subordinates could achieve in their own way. However they went about it and whatever traditions they pointed to as explanations for their eccentric behavior, the important thing was that the money was collected.   Never had the contradictions at the base of Austria's 'absolutism' been quite so manifest.[42]

That ambiguous position could not be maintained for long. By the middle of the summer of 1699 it became increasingly clear that the Hungarian administration would not be able to respond to the high expectations of the Austrian ministers. The cry want up now for the support of the Imperial army and for the deployment of that last of all resorts -- military execution. Before long it had become a not uncommon occurrence for the soldiers who had not been payed for months to receive their few gulden directly from the taxpayers without experiencing any need to call upon the intermediary offices of the War Commissariat, the Treasury, and the local authorities.[43]

Long before this point had been reached the convocation of Hungarian notables that had been convened on September 10, 1698, had been sent packing.[44] The Hungarian reaction to the demands of the Deputation had been expressed through official channels and with a determination that does not fail to arouse admiration. But the Hungarian magnates had not said all that was on their minds, when they sent their representatives to treat with the Deputation. One instance of the full range of their reaction can be found in an account of the convocation that was written many years afterwards by Prince Ferenc II Rákóczi. His memories were dominated by reports that the Austrian ministers planned to abolish the existing laws of Hungary, remove the remnants of the privileges of the nobility and the royal cities, and to establish a permanent appropriation, a *contributio continua*, that would excuse the ministers from the onerous duty of bargaining each year with the Hungarian leaders on the amount of the war-tax. These memories cannot be understood as an accurate description of the Deputation's goals -- even as these were conveyed to the members of the convocation. What was important here was Rákóczi's conviction that there was a definite plot against Hungary's traditional liberties, that this plot informed every proposal of the Deputation to the extent that mere supposition became transformed into fact.

A high point of this convocation was the interview granted by the Emperor to Archbishop Széchényi. The prelate, acting once again in his chosen role as a spokesman for the Hungarian notables, told the Emperor that they were unwilling to make any binding commitments without securing the formal approval of a Hungarian Diet. In Rákòczi's version of that meeting the Emperor was reported to have said that he fully agreed with Széchényi but that "his ministers had assured him that they could succeed by following the path they had taken; he simply wished to let them do this to see what the outcome would be." It is doubtful that Leopold would disavow the policy of his ministers in quite those terms, though he may have been guilty here of his usual practice of trying to make the best of a difficult situation by offering boundless assurances of goodwill and by disclaiming all responsibility for what was done in his name. On the day after the audience the Hungarian delegates demonstrated so violently for the summoning of the Diet, that the meetings of the convocation were prorogued. Leopold made his own views painfully clear, when he provided the Hungarian delegates, then in the process of returning to their *comitats*, with a striking expression of his displeasure. In an imperial rescript of December 24, 1698, he complained of the attitude of the nobles and assured them that he had no intention of permitting them to evade their obligations.

The spirits of the delegates were not noticeably depressed by their sudden dismissal and the Emperor's pointed expression of his disappointment at their attitude and conduct while in Vienna. They had no intention of yielding ground to the so-called "temporary expedients" of the Deputation, and their sudden removal from Vienna encouraged them to indulge once more in their habitual wishful thinking about the ancient constitution of Hungary. The conclusion of a peace with the Turks on January 26, 1699, provided them with additional ammunition for their contention that it was high time to restore the Hungarian status quo in its pristine form, and it was not long before the Palatine and the *Brevia brevium*, Hungary's highest tribunal, gave expression to this feeling in yet another set of proposals that was presented to the Emperor for his consideration.

This memorial was not discussed by the Deputation for once but by the Privy Conference. The reason for this change of venue had to do with the heavily constitutional nature of the proposals that were made. For once gulden took a secondary place, and Austrian officials found themselves struggling with more abstract notions. The meeting of the Conference on March 31, 1699, might be said to represent the views of the Deputation, since the members of the Conference were with one exception, the Lord High Chamberlain Count Waldstein, members of the Deputation as well, and the views they expressed fit neatly in with the general viewpoint that had evolved during the slightly more than one year of the Deputation's activity.[45] One missed Kinsky, of course (he had died the preceding month), and political discussion at so refined a level had narrowed down to the wit and wisdom of Harrach, Kaunitz, the elder Starhemberg, Bucceleni, and Kollonich.

The heart of the Hungarian demands were the following: the calling of a Hungarian Diet, the reuniting of Hungary with Transylvania, and a reduction both in the number of troops stationed in Hungary and in the size of the *contributio*. The majority of those present at the meeting (Kaunitz, Starhemberg, Bucceleni, and Kollonich) stoutly resisted the suggestion that the Emperor call the Hungarian Diet into session. They did not stoop to raise questions of principle; they obviously were afraid that the Hungarians would exceed the bounds of political good taste, if they were allowed to have their Diet, particularly if the Austrian government did not receive previous assurances that nothing untoward would occur in the course of the meetings -- the activities of the convocation in Vienna were too recent to permit the ministers to contemplate the spectacle of a full Diet at Bratislava with any degree of equanimity. In addition to his, Kaunitz and Kollonich were suspicious of the role of the *Brevia brevium* in formulating these proposals; they remembered that courts of this kind had frequently been sources of revolutionary acttvity in the past. It was the Conference's opinion that the Emperor should tell the Hungarians that he was too occupied with other problems at the moment -- this excuse had some foundation in truth because the problem of the Spanish succession absorbed more and more of his time and attention -- and that he would submit to them, when a favorable opportunity presented itself, a plan for the best reorganization of the Kingdom of Hungary. The ghost of the *Einrichtungswerk* had obviously not been laid to its final rest.

Austrian opposition to the proposed union of Hungary and Transylvania took a much milder form. In the *Diploma Leopoldinum* the Emperor had given his official blessing to the preservation of Transylvanian autonomy and its separation from Hungary. This policy of separation had been closely identified with Kinsky, but there were reasons for believing that the Transylvanians recognized the advantages accruing to them from their special status in the Monarchy. The *Diploma* clearly militated against reunion, though it could not be regarded as in any sense irrevocable. Starhemberg based his opposition to reunion on his belief that the political traditions of the two lands were so much at variance after a long period of separation that any fusion of the two would automatically result in an insurrection of the Transylvanians. Kollonich based his opposition on religious grounds; the union of Hungary and Transylvania would furnish the non-Catholics, who were prominent figures in the politics of tolerant Transylvania, with a chance to play a similarly important role in Hungarian politics, and he had no wish to see their influence extended to Hungary. For the time being, delay seemed to be the wisest course of action. The usual consolations were to be offered to the Hungarians; the promise might be made that there would be a reduction in the number of troops stationed in Hungary that would be consistent with the security requirements of the Emperor's dominions. But this was a wan hope indeed, since any drastic cutbacks in the size of the Habsburg military establishment was doomed to be vetoed by the very same men, acting in their other role as the Emperor's chief advisers in the field of foreign affairs.

The meeting of the Privy Conference had dealt with some of the fundamental questions of Hungary's relations with the rest of the Monarchy at a time when the Deputation faced the prospect of full-scale military executions in that country. Kollonich could worry about the virus of Transylvanian tolerance; he was equally capable of conducting a rigorous inspection of the tax registers of the Pozsony (Bratislava) *comitat* that had netted the information that, while seventeen hundred individuals had paid their taxes, seven hundred were still in default. The Primate's loving care was held up to the emulation of Austrian and Hungarian officials, but in the face of the growing financial crisis his way of doing things looked out of place.[46]

The Secretary had expressed the opinion that it was precisely on the outcome of its most ambitious undertaking, the new repartition, that the Deputation would stand or fall, "The Deputation should order another execution or it will prove that it is of absolutely no value whatsoever --which is in fact the case."[47] This view of the Deputation's work had not yet become general or had at least not been expressed by many of the members. But while the Secretary had the chance to make his views known within the context of the official record, the more prestigious members of the Deputation registered their opinions by absenting themselves from meetings. The Deputation had only been in existence a little more than a year, and it had suffered two fatal blows: the death of its first Chairman in Feburary 1698, and it failure to bring the Hungarians to terms. The struggle with Hungarian particularism had been carried on with a most unusual tenacity and will to have the last word, but the Hungarians have emerged the victors. Their victory pointed to the decline of the Deputation as a force in Austrian affairs, but this victory had not been just another Hungarian victory over the zealots of Austrian 'absolutism'. In its most profound significance the victory had been won by the traditional view of society that considered it axiomatic that everything "depends on the vote of supply of the local diet."[48] The Secretary who said this may well have had his reservations about the practice, but there can be no doubt that he believed it to be a foundation of the Austrian Monarchy's political life that not even the Emperor could afford to erode. If for any reason, and he was well aware that the financial crisis might be considered reason enough, the Emperor were to override this system, he would be guility of a tactical error and, in addition, would gain very little from his transgression against the established order of things: such a move "would produce just as little as has been secured before."[49] It was the hold upon even so lively a mind as this of the political traditions of the *Ständestaat* that was the key to the Deputation's failure to resolve the Hungarian dilemma.

Notes

1. Wellmann, "Merkantilistische Vorstellungen im 17. Jahrhundert und Ungarn," *Nouvelles etudes historiques* (Budapest, 1965), I, 341-342.

2. O. Redlich, *Geschichte Österreichs* (Gotha, 1921), VI, 537-538.

3. The monograph of Theodor Mayer, *Verwaltungsreform in Ungarn nach der Türkenzeit* (Wien, 1911), is the best introduction to a study of the *Einrichtungswerk*; it contains the complete text in the "Anhang", pp. I-XLV. Oswald Redlich has a lengthy discussion, *op. cit.*, VI, 537-546. The best modern treatment by a Hungarian historian is surely the article of Wellmann, *loc. cit.*, I, 315-354.

4. For a dissenting view on the sincerity of Leopold I's interest in improving the condition of the peasantry, particularly in Hungary, cf. A. Varkonyi, "Habsburg Absolutism and Serfdom in Hungary at the Turn of the 17th and 18th Centuries," *ibid.*, 355-387.

5. Mayer felt that the *Einrichtungswerk* established the fact that "der Wiener Hof in semen socialen, wirtschaftlichen und kulturellen Ansichten ausserordentlich hoch stand...", *op. cit.*, 80.

6. "Conclusum: Ihr May. vorzustellen, das heut von zwey haubtpunkten tractirt: Primo de stabiliendo fundo der 12 millionen. Secundo die mittel zur anticipation zu finden. Ad primum quia fundus 12 millionen ex puns tributis provinciarum conflueret, den ietzigen standt des contributionswesens in iedem landt zu überlegen und zu sehen, wo es haffte, durch was mittl und weg es zu stabiliren.", *Deputationaprotokoll 1698* (hereafter *Dep. Prot. 1698*) Feb. 14, fol. 100-101.

7. "Ratione Hungariae dass bisherigen unbilligen modi, quod in tribus consistat, befunden: 1. Dass in das contributionswesen clerus, magnas, nobilis, civis et subditus pro viribus facultatum gleich eingezogen. 2. Die accisen eingeführet. 3. Die repartition ehistens verfertiget, anhero gesendet und das verflossene monath assignirt werden", *ibid.*, fol. 100.

8. "...idque sine mora, quia forte ab remissum frigus subditi fugerent et repartitio una cum 4 millionibus posset impossibilitari.", a view expressed at the same session, *ibid.*, fol. 101.

9. "Herr Cardinal: in Lingarn zu gehen seye umbsonst, si non habeamus pecuniam. Dixisset mense Maio, das man vorhero das geld haben müesse... *Ungarn thue mehr, alss es versprochen, unterhalte die gantze armada* (italics my own). Zwey millionen wären auff die pauern und die stettiache repartirt. Zwey solle man auff den clerum und die nobiles schiagen"; the Cardinal realized in the midst of his optimistic mood that a collection of this kind might well have to be carried out *vi et armis*: "...dass sie mit verweilung der militz und commissariats dahin zu gehen, die repartition zu erzwingen.

Item zur eintreibung des benöthigten sich gebrauchen könten.", *ibid.*, Feb. 20, 1698, fol. 103-106 passim.

10. "Legitur memoriale domini Palatini...; 1. Repartitio. 2. Reglement.
3. Gleichheit der contribution; Concluditur: Rescribendum Palatino, dass dergleichen mit Ihr. May. dienst nicht bestehen (könne), die comitatus cum omnibus incolis sive sit clerus sive nobilis sive rusticus sive civis in ein gleiches mitleiden zu ziehen und zu beobachten, *das der schwechere von dem sterckheren übertragen werde* (italics my own), *ibid.*, fol. 117-118 (the date of the session is uncertain but it must have taken place in early March 1698.)

11. "Respondit dominus Palatinus, quod regnicolae viderint se impares
residuiis 2 millionibus et speraverint relaxationem... (Kinsky in his conclusion)." Ita etiam respectu qualis kein unterschied inter provincias. Die bewilligung wäre Ihr. May. aigens gueth; die modi administrandi rem propriam iuxta propriam convenientem zu bestellen, und seye as an deme, das Ihr. May. von dieser Ihrer gerechtigkeit ohne praeiuditz Ihrer höchsten authoritet darvon nicht weichen konte.", *ibid.*, same session, fol. 164.

12. "Ihr Eminenz: Die Ungarn wären den 6. nachmittags beysammengewiesen und (hätten) geschlossen, man sofle die vorige 2 millionen doppelt anlegen und per executionem einbringen. Budiani putasset, ess würde einen auffstand veruhrsachen. Dominus Cardinalia etiam iudicasset iniquum.", *ibid.*, May 9, 1698, fol. 153.

13. Ibid., fol. 154

14. "Legitur resolutio Caesarea ad Ungaros: Quad nihil potuerit relaxari
de 4 millionibus et nullas amplius replices admittere velit. Iagitur dass Kay. billet, lauth dessen Ihr. Kay. dem auffsatz der resolution, welche denen Ungarn zu eröfnen, appropirt. NB: Est ibi his verbis: Acceptare Suam Sanctam Mtem grato animo, quad praefati domini, Primas, Palatinus et magnates 4 milliones spatia 12 mensium integre persolvendos susceperint etc. etc.", *ibid.* "Sessio 46," probably in the middle of May 1698, fol. 156.

15. *Ibid.*, same session, fol. 157.

16. "Dominus Cardinalis dicit, es werde der arme man da doppelt belegt, wan die perceptores ihre register nicht einschickhen theten, dass man sehe, wer contribuire und wer nicht contribuire, werde man nicht auff den grund kommen." This *votum* was followed by some very reasonable comments from the Secretary: "Zuzuwarthen bis particulariter alles ex comitatibus komme, brauchte viel zeit. Registra ex comitatibus zu erwarthen würde gar zu lang hergehen.", *ibid.*, June 2, 1698, fol. 162.

17. "Herr graff von Starhemberg resentit hoc, item dominus Aulae
Cancellarius. Khamen hart aneinander. Dominus Kinsky inquit insurgens, die Bucceleni wären bissig.", *ibid.*, same session, fol. 162.

18. "Intuitu dessen Ihr May. saepius ex parte Deputationis repraesentirt, wie nöthig seye, durchgehendts die erbländer in den nöthigen beytrag zu den 12 millionen zu proportioniren und gleich zu halten, quae petitio reitaretur, quia esset ad conservandum scepter und cron, landt und leuth...." *Ibid.*, fol. 163.

19. "Resolutio Caesarea: Was dass von meinem erbländern begehrte quantum anlanget, werde ich fest darob halten, dass solches auff ein oder andere weis oder weg von jedem landt eingehen solle. In deme ich in meinen ländern keine ungleichheit zulassen kan."; "Dominus Kinsky: Nemo deberet ease exemptu modus collectandi autem denen comitatibus gelassen." *Ibid.*, June 6, 1698, fol. 164.

20. "Dominus Kinsky proposuit de conventu Hungarorum, so dahier scm solle. Dominus Cardinalis: Frustra hic conveniret. Werde viehl kosten. Der modus contribuendi seye nicht in einem comitatu wie in den anderen. Respondetur, Caesarem velle, ut conveniant", *ibid.*, June 23, 1698, fol. 175

21. The Deputation discussed a report that had been submitted to it on conditions in Transylvania sometime at the end of August (the exact date of the meeting is not known), *ibid.*, fol. 204-205.

22. "Legatur memoriale Palatini et procerum Hungariac, quo petunt, cum eleges statuant, ut negotia regni non tractentur extra regnum, ut deliberatio super communicata puncta remittatur Posonium.... Propositiones regnum concernentes tractandae per modum dieetae allegant decreta von 150 jahren her, die viehlleicht in einen anderen standt gerathen. Sie haben sich selbst eingelassen und propositiones übergeben. Nuper interrogaverunt, quorsum registra. *Ansam huius postulati dabit, quod magnates non contribuerint, imo eingenommen* (italics my own). Si remittatur Posoniam, nihil fiet." *Ibid.*, Sept. 18,
1698, fol. 216.

23. "Dominus comes Kinsky concludit: Man solle denen Ungarn repraesentiren, dass die materia ex necessitate per compendium tractirt werden müesse. Es hetten Ihr May. kein intention, Ungariae status in ihren privilegiis zu khränckhen, wohl aber dem ex discordia regni leidenden königlich zu einer gleichheit zu verhelffen", *ibid.*, same session, fol. 216.

24. "Status ipsimet desiderarent cum caeteris provinciis aequaliter tractari. Unde etiam vocarentur ad aulam provinciales salvis tamen legibus fundamentalibus.... Alias Caesar ipsemet cogeretur disponere.", *ibid.*, same session, fol. 217.

25. "Deinde nullam exemptionem cuiuscunque personae commodum in regno percipientis inveniendum, sed omnes et singulos pro qualitate facultatum in sustentationis onus trahendos. Dicendum etiam, dass man sie vor erörterung dieser sachen nit weglassen werde... omnia itaque haec cum ministerio Suae Mtis. Proinde opus

esse, ut ipsimet omnia accelerent.", *ibid.*, Sept. 22, 1698, fol. 218.

26. *Ibid.*, Oct. 20, 1698, fol. 230.

27. "Starenberg: Die rebellen, so nach Monkatz kommen, non conquerentur contra Caesarem, non contra militem Germanum, sed contra dominos.", *ibid.*, same session, fol. 231.

28. This view was probably expressed by the Secretary, *ibid.*, same session, fol. 231.

29. "Dominus Palm: Die Hungarn hetten eine geidrepartition gemacht,
die nit richtig. Dicit Palm dass geld müesse da sein.... Ad memorialem Palati (sic.) dicendum, das auff ihnen die schuld ligge, das man kein ordnung gehalten habe..... Das contributions quantum also auszutheilen, das 2/3 auff den unterthanen und 1/3 auff den herren zu legen.", *ibid.*, same session, fol. 232.

30. "Dominus Kaunitz: Cum incerta pax, wären die leuth noch zu behalten.... Man solle doch die obere stände nicht disgustiren: Nur von diesem jahrzu sagen.", *ibid.*, Oct. 27, 1698, fol. 233.

31. "Etiam videndum, dass man ihnen metum perpetuitatis benemme und sage, der modus sage, der modus werde bleiben, bis sie einen besseren an die hand geben"; "Wass da wohl auffgesetzt werde sine vi ooactiva nit ad effectum zu bringen sein. Et sicut absque ho modo non apud provinciam, ita etiam non sine vi apud militiam"-- the conclusum on Oct. 27, 1698, *ibid.* fol. 234-235.

32. "Palatini memoriale: Quod intellexerit tertiam partem solvendam
esse a clero et nobilitate. Non speraret intentionem hanc esse Suae Mtis., ut nobilitas pereat.... Vix octo comitatus integros mansisse in Ungaria ab anno 1662, dum Turca Varadinum occupassent. A quo tempore Turca fugatus, nullum respirium affulsisset. Immensum contributionis onus impositum. Plebs et nobilis in eandem devolverentur perditionem", *ibid.*, Nov. 12, 1698, fol. 242.

33. In the *conclusum* of the same session: "Sunt argumenta tamen ad
specialem (?) ponderosa. Magnae calamitates in Ungaria.... Potius suavitate quam per violentiam", *ibid.*, fol. 242.

34. "Dominus Kinsky: Placuisse quidezn Suae Mti., ut audiantur. Interea standum prioribus decretis", *ibid.* Nov. 13, 1698, fol. 242.

35. *Ibid.*, same session, fol. 243

36. "Dominus Palatinus dicit, quod semper ipsi fecerint repartitionem... Quoad clerum et nobiles haec modalitas suaderetur, ut in triiesima parte concurrent -- essent 133,333 aut loco tricesimac de centum -- ex proventibus tres.", *Ibid.*, Nov. 14, 1698, fol. 244.

37. "Fit computum von denen 4 millionen: 16. pars: 250. 000 fl.;
30. pars: 133. 000 fl; manerent: 3.061.666 fl. *Ibid.*, same session, fol. 244.

38. "Dominus Kaunitz :   ...Tertialitatem werde man nicht erhalten. Vermeinet das
duplum, wass die stette geben. Nimirum octavam partem." *Ibid*, fol. 246.

39. "Legitur memoriale dominorum Hungarorum contra octavalitatem: Petunt reduci
ad 24. partem." *Ibid.*, Nov. 17, 1698, fol. 247.

40. "Der arme mann wirt die 3.500.000 fl. nicht geben können....
Conclusum zu sagen, hic et nunc könne man es nicht Indern. Ess seye auff keine
perpetuitet angesehen. Der gemeine man habe den last allein getragen. Mit dem brod
wolle man doch dispensiren", *ibid.*, same session, fol. 247.

41. As, for example, the complaints of Kosice, which were discussed
at some length, *Dep. Prot. 1699*, Jan. 2, 1699, fol. 2.

42. Kollonich declared at the same session that he was unable to advise
the Emperor to order an execution in Upper Hungary, *ibid*, fol. 3.

43. "Commissariatus erindert, man solle den regimentern in Ungarn die
quittung an die comitatus geben und ihre anweisungen selbst eiubringen lassen", *ibid.*,
April 6, 1699, fol. 21, but this was probably too roundabout. The result was the excesses
which the Deputation felt it had to consider in some detail.

44. This convocation has not been studied in detail, though it has
played an interesting role in historiographical controversy. The one source that has
evoked interest is Rákòczi's *Histoire des revolutions de Hongrie* (The Hague, 1735),
140ff. But the accuracy of his account has been challenged by Mayer, *op. cit.* , 113-115,
who has some success in establishing the fact that the Prince was not speaking as an
eyewitness and that his testimony was that of an elderly man recalling events in his
youth.

45. The discussion of the meeting of the Privy Confrence is based on the "Protokoll
einer Sitzung der Geheimen Konferenz ueher die Forderung der Ungarn, einen Reichstag
abzuhalten, Siebenbuergen mit Ungarn zu vereinigen, die Zahl der in Ungarn stationierten
Truppen zu verringern und die Steuern zu senken," *Vortäge*, March 31, 1699 (Fasz. 37,
Mappe II), fol. 21-26.

46. *Dep. Prot. 1699*, April 23, fol. 22-24.

47. "Der Deputation eine andere execution einzuräumen oder sie seye
nichts nutz, quod *verum* est (word underlined in cipher)", *ibid.*, Jan. 29, 1699, fol. 8.

48. *Ibid.*, May 18, 1699, fol. 27.

49. *Ibid.*, same session, fol. 27. The Secretary's remarks were marginal notes to the opinion of Count Gundacker Starhemberg who had argued for a stabilization of the *contributio* which ran counter to the system then in existence of *postulata* and the *Bewilligungen*.

Chapter Seven
Conclusum / Summation

"Conclusum: Man konne bey dieser session noch nichts stabiliren. Die ausgab übertreffe den empfang. Man seye auch nit versichert, das die länder alles thun werden oder können.... Sehe also nit, wie auszukommen seye.... Ad cameram denique."
Deputationsprotokoll 1700

The Deputation's responsibility for administering the new and badly mangled tax system continued throughout 1699. Its humbling experience in working out the details of the Hungarian repartition for 1699 may well have been intensely educational, but this did not mean that the committee would be in any better position when it negotiated the repartition for 1700. In October 1699, the Emperor sent the Hungarian Chancellor to the Deputation's Chairman Count Harrach with a report that the Palatine had intended to work out the details of the next repartition with the assistance of a number of Hungarian magnates who were in Vienna at the time. But this informal group of advisers had refused to cooperate with him on the pretext that they wished to avoid any further responsibility for a settlement of the tax question that might produce an unfavorable reaction in Hungary. They had suggested that the Kingdom of Hungary be divided along conventional regional lines and that the resulting six parts -- Transdanubia, Cisdanubia, Upper Hungary, Transtibiscia, Croatia, and Slavonia -- be enpowered to send representatives to Vienna for a conference on the repartition.[1] The inclusion of Croatia and Slavonia was not to be wondered at, for it was the traditional Hungarian view that the events of the past century and a half had not altered the boundaries of the Kingdom of St. Stephen. From a practical standpoint this might mean that a slightly larger group of taxpayers would be expected to perform the *salto mortale* of meeting Hungary's excessive tax obligations. The Austrian ministers did not immediately protest; any mention of Croatia and Slavonia made them uncomfortable, since they were not at all certain of the exact legal status of these areas. But Kollonich had been more interested by the suggestion that there be yet another conference. Remembering the unpleasant experiences of the autumn of 1698, he made it quite clear that he wished to avoid any repetition of that debacle. The committee finally parried this latest Hungarian thrust by sending the proposal back to the Palatine with the request that he, the Hungarian Chancellor, and the resident magnates confer on this matter.[2]

It had not seen the end of proposals by the Hungarians, for shortly afterwards the Palatine presented them with yet another memorial. Here the Hungarians said that they had hoped that the return of peace would bring with it the end of emergency measures and the re-establishment of their constitutional rights and privileges, particularly the exemption of the nobility from taxation. They were now shocked to be told that their Palatine was once again involved in the business of parcelling out the taxes in a way that they could only interpret as the conversion of a wartime expedient into standard official practice. They expressed the hope that the Enperor's ministers would understand their misgivings about the legality of taxing the nobility "as if it belonged to the common herd."[3] Once that point had been made they referred once again to their desire to see Croatia, Slavonia, and the *comitats* of the *Neoacquistica*, an area that had been withdrawn from the territory under the Palatine's control, which had not figured in the previous repartition should be included in the one that was now under consideration.

The remaining proposals in the memorial took issue with the practice of selling estates in the *Neoacquistica* (the Treasury had been engaged in fairly extensive sales of what they believed to be Hungarian real estate) or of making presents of such properties to deserving ministers and generals, even to the Palatine himself, as the Hungarian Chancellery had been doing. It was time now, said the memorial, to return these estates to those individuals who could establish a claim to legal ownership.[4] The overall inpression created by such a document was that the Hungarians were continuing to harp on an all too familiar theme: the Austrians should allow Hungary to return to its traditional ways -- geographically, constitutionally, socially. All these customs and rights revolved around one thing, however, the preservation of the privileged position of the clergy, the magnates, and the gentry.

The members of the Deputation showed no enthusiasm for the memorial or for a continuation of the debate with such insistent antagonists. Their *vota* were unimaginative and dispirited. Croatia, it was allowed, did fall under the historic jurisdiction of Hungary, but no one wished to draw any practical conclusions from that admission. The best that could be managed for the Hungarians was the promise that the points that had been raised would be discussed at a later date.[5]

These first inconclusive rounds in the match between Hungary and the Deputation led into talks that followed the desultory pattern which had been established in 1698. The failure to come anywhere near the target of twelve million gulden forced the government to lower its sights; the new *fundus* was ten million gulden, and the Hungarian quota was set at 3,200,000 gulden, which was virtually the same percentage it had been expected to pay the previous year. The finale of this set of negotiations had an air of improvisation that could not hide the government's fear that even the new sum ran far beyond the Hungarians' ability to pay. The Court was busy with its preparations for Christmas, when the Deputation set down these figures as final. It asked the Palatine to look after the details and tried to comfort the Hungarians with the cheerless assurance that everyone would be happier if His Imperial Majesty could be more permissive when it came to the *contributio* but his continuing financial difficulties (they showed no signs of abating) left him no alternative but to insist on the figure that had been quoted. The reports from Madrid became more disquieting with the arrival of every courier, and Hungary was urged to have patience. Patience at this time and in regard to the tax would ensure that it would receive concessions -- unspecified of course -- in less critical areas of public concern. The haste with which all this was done probably sprang from a reluctance to allow the Hungarians to say anything more than that they would acquiesce under pressure.[6]

In the first years of its work the Deputation had managed to carry the day with its jealously-guarded *fundus*. The sums had been preserved, and the Hungarians had been brought around to accepting them at least on paper. But the effort to relieve the economic pressure on the *misera plebs* had been crowned not with apparent success but with ignominious failure. The plan that had been a mixture of compassion and realism (the upper orders in Hungary were more likely to have the money to pay the tax) had envisaged an easy division into two million gulden for the clergy and the nobles and two million gulden for the peasants. Such a plan may have been convincing to the Emperor and his ministers, but at the first rude contact with Hungarian reality it had suffered a blow from which it would never recover.

Slowly and with the utmost reluctance the Deputation had been required to sacrifice its illusions and to work for an accomodation with the powerful in Hungary. Vienna's empty treasury drove it to devise a new tax system and to create a committee to superintend its functioning; it also made it an absolute necessity to compromise with the Hungarians. This balance was achieved at the end of a long set of negotiations, and it gave no sign of being anything other than a precarious one. No decree, no agreement, no understanding in this strange conflict between Vienna and the Hungarian nobles could be regarded as final. The moment the Deputation felt that it had had the last word and the Hungarians had been reduced to silence the argument would continue in a slightly different way. One moment it was all facts and arithmetical sums, the next full of constitutional theory and well-contrived memories of a glorious past. The list of points that could be made by the Hungarians even under the greatest duress should have aroused the grudging admiration of the men to whom the Hungarian talking points had become so familiar.

If the Deputation could not be rudely dismissed as a failure on the basis of the first two years there can be no doubt that it had fallen far short of the Emperor's most sanguine expectations. The experiment, perhaps the last experiment, that the aging Leopold made had not been a success. But even failure of the kind experienced by this committee did not condemn it immediately to dissolution. It continued its work, though with far less sense of urgency and with agendas given over to the administrative area of its official interest. Hungary having proven to be far too much of a problem, it was the most natural of reactions to see if something could be salvaged at a lower level, at a level at which the members felt more at home. This is not to say that Hungary no longer asked for attention, but, as if to suggest that the Hungarians had no wish to underline the extent of their triumph, the cases that came before the committee now were largely lists of grievances from the *comitats*.[7] Case after case followed in a sickening succession of military excesses, thefts, corrupt practices, even mutinies. And even though old Starhemberg grumbled that the members should remember that his "soldiers are not monks" the Deputation managed at least to convey its sense of outrage.

Kollonich, much criticized for his loyalty to the dynasty's cause rather than to purely Hungarian interests, made a characteristic effort to see that amends were made to those who had suffered and that the guilty parties were punished. In a case involving an officer, both he and the Secretary insisted that the good name of the Emperor was at stake and that any connivance in a miscarriage of justice would have a most profound and disastrous effect on Hungarian affection for their Kind.[7a] And then there was the tragicomic 'Affair of the Cow's Feet'. An officer, quartered with a family of German peasants in Hungary, had suddenly developed an appetite for baked calf's foot one evening. The peasants had been unable or unwilling to provide him with this delicacy, when he had asked them to do so, and the officer had dispatched his orderly to the barn with orders to chop off the feet of the German's innocent cows. The Deputation expressed great indignation at the report of such an atrocity; it ordered the payment of compensation, and those members who were not military men had a field day with their complaints that the soldiers were guilty of committing innumerable acts of folly that made very little sense. The 'Affair of the Cow's Feet' symbolized a very dangerous trend. That a body of the alleged importance of the Deputation should devote itself to such considerations testified at once to a desire for justice and to a loss of the will to play a great role in Austrian affairs. It had taken refuge finally in minutiae, and in that limbo it was destined to remain for the balance of its collective existence.

> Conclusion: We are still not going to put things into order this time. Expenditures are greater than income. We are also not even certain that the lands will or can do everything in their power. The War Council says that we have to have an army because of the dangerous situation. The Treasury says that this is not possible; the *contributio* is uncertain and don't cover the costs in any event. It is impossible to see how we can find our way out of this fix. If one diverts some of the funds for our creditors then the army has to go without. Refer it to the Treasury as a last resort.[8]

The Deputation had found its epitaph, a cry from the heart of bureaucrats, soldiers, and ecclesiastics who could no longer imagine any manner of escape from their plight that was not miraculous. The iron law of insufficient funds, mutinous soldiers, and Hungarians in insurrection had begun to assert itself; it proved too powerful for the Deputation that had sought in its more hopeful moments to rise above such grim considerations. But even from its first moments there had been those warnings of what was to come. "...soldiers are always an absolute necessity in Hungary... it takes only a small band of rebels to set the whole country into motion."[9] The danger increased, of course, when Leopold began to make his preparations in earnest for the conflict with France over the Spanish Succession, and when the war came at the beginning of 1701 it forced the Austrians to transfer regiments from Hungary to the front that had opened up in Italy. At that very time, Count Starhemberg reminded the Deputation that "all signs point to a rebellion in Hungary and so we can't possibly denude that country of troops."[10] The crisis of 1683 seemed to be repeating itself, though this time the prospects were even bleaker.[11] The members of the Deputation were well aware of the threat of an insurrection, and when it did come in 1703 under the leadership of Prince Rákóczi no one who knew anything at all about the context in which the Deputation had operated could regard it as a surprise. Though they were not surprised they did not respond with any great show of decision. This apparent apathy had serious consequences, and it would raise question in some minds about the quality of Austrian leadership in the face of a real threat to the survival of the Austrian Monarchy.[12] Apathy played a part in this distressing performance, and old age, too, but even the Mansfelds, the Salaburgs, the Harrachs of that small world can be forgiven for a display of fatalism in the presence of forces they could not even pretend to control. Then it was that Leopold I received the gift of yet another 'miracle' -- the intelligence, the energy, the drive in men like Eugene of Savoy, Gundacker Starhemberg, Johann Wenzel Wratislaw who were at last permitted to assume key positions in his government. But these 'new men', if they managed to bring the Monarchy through one of its worse crises, came too late to be able to save the Deputation.

The fate of the Deputation was closely tied to the older generation of Austrian ministers, to men who had been in their mature years when the Turks attacked Vienna and in their sixties when asked to assist the Emperor in his latest administrative venture, a coordinating committee designed to rid his government of some of the confusions for which they were partly responsible. They had participated as representatives of the *collegia* and had defended the views of these bodies with varying degrees of success. They had not failed to be very much in character as individuals: Kinsky, Kaunitz, Kollonich, Starhemberg, and the Secretary had left their personal imprints on the proceedings and, to some extent, the inevitable outcome of all their discussion. But they had spoken as men who were divided by their perspectives in Austrian internal affairs, by factional loyalties that were less publicized than the Court parties and yet in some ways of far greater importance. A close reading of the minutes of the Deputation's meetings indicates that there were probably four fairly distinct views on internal policy operative there.

Of the original members, Kaunitz, Kollonich, and Gundacker Starhemberg (a somewhat later arrival, though he had represented the ailing Breuner as early as February 1698) displayed an interest in reform carried out along the lines of rationalisation of the administration and the centralisation of political power. But within this general tendency there were noticeable differences in emphasis. Kaunitz spoke for a 'Bohemian' position. He believed that all the Emperor's dominions should be treated alike in the expectation that Bohemia would benefit from the equalisation of the taxes, etc. After all it was Bohemia that had been carrying the greatest part of the financial burden, and when someone like Kaunitz reiterated the slogan of "Each land should be treated like the others" he rarely went much beyond that point. What was wanted was tax relief and an end to favoritism, the pampering of one of the lands at the expense of the others. The slogan and the position it typified did not espouse a radical policy of gathering power into the hands of the officials at Vienna, but it paradoxically attacked local interests in the name of one particular local interest, and to that extent it deserved to be included in the move, however tentative it might be, for reform.[13]

Kollonich had his own position, of course, and after removing the obvious eccentricities that were so frequent in his expression of his views it could be described quite accurately as a 'Hungarian' version of the Bohemian position. He believed that Hungary must do its part as a working member of the Habsburg system (often he seemed to be saying that it should do more than its part) and that it must be brought into line with the Austrian and the Bohemian Lands without being made to feel that it had been penalized for some major infraction of the rules. This still allowed him to resent attempts to deny the Hungarians equal treatment even though he had to admit that due respect must be shown for local conditions. God after all had not made Styria flat.[14] That was a fact of geography that could not be overlooked, a fact as evident as the acknowledged variations in local constitutional law and practice. Most of the time Kollonich acted as the watchdog for the *misera plebs*; indeed, the Hungarian peasants had no more concerned an advocate in Vienna than their Primate whose devotion to the Hungarian status quo continued to leave something to be desired.

For he extended the principle of equality to the various classes of Hungarian society to the degree that by such a radical innovation the status and the economic condition of the peasants would be improved. The Cardinal felt that there were eminently practical grounds for the proposed official intervention on their behalf; it was his view that a few thousand peasants could do far more harm to the government than a few nobles who received so much more attention and whose activities were followed with trepidation and fear.[15]   Yet this highly idiosyncratic 'Hungarian' position failed to argue very strongly for centralization.   It wavered to a far greater degree than the Bohemians did between the two poles of the central and the local governments, but it, too, sought to avail itself of the doctrine of equality to ameliorate conditions in one part of the Monarchy. In Kollonich's case the goal was an improvement of conditions in Hungary; in their case it was a better share for the Bohemians.

The young Gundacker von Starhemberg may have been the only individual who had the interest and the intelligence that was needed for the development of a forthright policy of centralization of the Habsburg lands. He knew how urgent reform had become with the deepening of the government's financial crisis; he was literally forced to speak up for improvements in taxation and, as a necessary corollary to that, the strengthening of the whole fabric of Austrian administration.   He thought that it was reasonable to determine the *fundus* by estimating the expenses for the coming fiscal year; he had openly spoken for the introduction of a universal income tax and the establishment of long-term votes of supply by the Diets that would free the offices in Vienna of much worry and uncertainty.[16]

These varied expressions of interest in reform closely paralleled movements that could be discerned in other European countries. Necessity and not a sudden outburst of political theorizing explained much of this polarization to reform. Necessity had been the obvious parent of the advanced notions of the younger Starhemberg, but necessity could not of itself provide him, financial expert that he was, with the mmkings of a grand political design.[17] In moments of deepest crisis, he could secure a grudging acceptance of parts of his program, as, for example, in the case of the Emperor's adoption of an income tax in the face of complete bankruptcy. The threat of imminent disaster might push old and indecisive men into a posture of modernity, but they had little enthusiasm for the pose and no conviction that it would have successful results. Starhemberg had to expect that his youth would work to the disfavor of the proposals he made. In the eyes of most members of the Deputation they were inextricably connected to his junior position and lack of experience, and he, too, had been guilty of placing an additional burden on the Treasury that he felt needed so much reorganization. A special grant had to be made by the Emperor to cover his debts, and the report of this act of kindness aroused the ire of old Count Öttingen and the envy of the Palatine, whose appetite for money and property surely exceeded that of the temporary Director of the Treasury.[18]

The remainder of the Deputation tended to be consistent in their defence of the traditional order of local custom and law in the Austrian and the Bohemian Lands. This defence, indeed, placed its emphasis on the special position of the Austrian Lands and even went so far as to support the notion that the very heart of the Monarchy geographically and psychologically speaking should be given preferential treatment. These men spoke as Austrians from above or below the Enns, and their closeness to the Emperor and their intimate knowledge of his affairs had only served to convince them that the old ways were always the best. Though they had risen to positions of undoubted eminence at Court and in the administrative system of the Austrian Monarchy they could be quite as programmatic as the 'egalitarians' in making an axiom of the belief that the "constitutions of the lands are not the same, and it would be quite impossible to alter them in any way." And if such an attempt was made they were convinced that the Emperor would be guilty of breaking his pledges to his subjects and that he would then be responsible for dragging himself and the dynasty and the lands he ruled down to general ruin.[20] This stout defence of the traditionalist position made no effort to be complete, for it showed surprising malleability in contemplating some degree of change in Hungary. This could not be set down simply to hypocrisy or to callow disregard of the traditions of another people; they did come under the general rubric of traditions, but from the standpoint of the 'Austrian' party they were traditions too old and obsolete to merit their complete support. Hungarian conditions seemed outmoded even by their conservative standards, and they had a case of sorts in urging that Hungary agree to do its part by assuming some of the terrible burden of supporting the Austrian war machine.

It was only natural that this devotion to the letter of the law when combined with a recognition of the pressing needs of the moment led them to indulge in maneuvers which sought to preserve the legal appearances while modification of governmental practice was taking place. But this kind of ambiguity was repulsive to them, and eventually the Austrians' sense of guilt began to assert itself, a development that was made even more inevitable by the failure of the reforming policies that had been pushed with such energy in the first enthusiastic moments of the Deputation's existence. When the true measure of defeat became clear and innovation had suffered a real setback, the traditionalists, the Austrians, pressed home their advantage by criticizing the whole effort that had been made to improve the situation. Count Mansfeld acted as their spokesman when, at a meeting of the Privy Conference, he summed up the reactions of the older generation to the policies that had been so hopefully embodied in the Deputation:

> They have placed far too much trust in their twelve millions, hoping in this way for miracles and realizing only after some time had passed that their plan was just not practical. The proponents of such measures wish to imitate France without first determining whether or not that system is possible or even practical here. It is their novelties that are responsible for the fact that the old ways have been completely abandoned and the army is in a state of complete ruin.[21]

Mansfeld was surely overstating his case, but it is interesting to note his attempt to further weaken the position of those who favored innovation by tagging them with the guilt of imitating the French. The Emperor would be quick to react negatively to any suggestion that the policies pursued by his government were French in inspiration. While no one can doubt that the French system was certainly à la mode in much of Europe, no one can be sure that the French example had been decisive in establishing the *fundus* or the Deputation, for that matter. The Emperor's response to a statement of the kind made by Mansfeld is not known, though it is permissible to suspect that Leopold would have agreed in principle with his old crony. The Emperor's mind told him that improvements were necessary if the governmental machinery was to survive the inordinate strains of war and internal dissension, and he was quite capable of lending his authority and prestige to a programme like that developed in the *Ordnung und Instruction*. But when that reform, partial and tentative though it was, encountered strong opposition Leopold retreated to the security of the traditional order of things and allowed the hopeful innovation to be sabotaged by the incompetence and the lack of reforming conviction of his oldest and closest collaborators.

* * *

Each session of the Deputation ended with the *conclusum*, the summation of the meeting by the Chairman or the Acting Chairman, and it is only appropriate to provide a similar summing-up of this brief study of the Deputation. Though it would require the talent of a Kinsky to list all the potentialities inherent in the institution and the consequences of its activity a few salient facts do emerge. The Deputation deserves a small yet significant place in the complex evolution of the Austrian central administration. In its principal role as a coordinating committee of the chief offices and agencies of that administrative apparatus it sought to improve the speed and the quality of Austria's response to its new status as a Great Power. In the manner of previous deputations, subcommittees of the Privy Council or the Privy Conference, it concerned itself with a particular problem -- in this case the financial and political aspects of the Austrian war machine. Though much of its work had revolved around taxation and especially the willingeess or unwillingness of the Hungarians to pay a much larger war-tax it cannot claim to be Austria's "first permanent conference on financial affairs"; it did not pretend to permanence and there were large areas of finance that did not come into its discussions.[22]

The Deputation pointed up the growing obsolescence of Austria's network of consultative councils and collegial bodies. In essence it acted as an official shortcut to administrative consensus and the quick and certain execution of policies agreed upon by the chiefs of the major Austrian offices. As such it was an expedient developed to handle a particular situation, and once it had tried its luck it would either receive further encouragement, if successful, or be allowed to retire slowly and imperceptibly from the limelight, as was in fact to be the case.

The Deputation also pointed to a future in which the great work of government would be undertaken by a cabinet or ministerial council. It had brought the most important ministers together in a common cause and had given evidence of a sort that the next stage in the development of the governmental structure would find the monarch dispensing with unwieldy consultative councils and relying more and more on close collaboration with a few ministers or secretaries. The road to full-fledged ministerial government was to be interminable in Austria; it did not put in an official appearance until the revolutionary year of 1848. But in its own limited way the Deputation had contributed to that line of development.

The role of the Deputation in Austrian institutional history raises a question as to whether or not institutions similar to it are to be found in other parts of Europe. The answer to that question is as difficult as any in the comparative study of European administration, but certain interesting similarities do appear. Spain, for example, witnessed the development of *juntas* in the early seventeenth century, and they, too, could be considered proof that the conciliar system that had reached a particularly high state of development in Spain had begun to decline in a most serious and troubling way.[23] Indeed, wherever the councils were too hidebound or too slow to respond, 'deputations' in fact if not in name made their appearance. France witnessed the development of *comités* of ministers in the reign of Louis XV. The full session of the *Conseil d' Etat* under the presidency of the King did not give the ministers sufficient opportunity to develop policies, and they had continual recourse to preparatory meetings or to committees that concerned themselves with one set problem over a period of time.[24] In Prussia, too, an atmosphere like that surrounding the creation of the Deputation existed just before Frederick William I created the *General-Ober-Finanz-Kriegs-und Domainen-Direktorium*. The Hohenzollern felt the need for a greater degree of coordination of the Prussian General Finance Directory with the general war commissariat. It was a measure of the great gifts of that difficult man that he did not stop short at the creation of a body like our Deputation but went further on to the more fundamental combination of the civil and military administration into one body.[25]

The most powerful single reason for improvisation of this kind may well have been the need to face roughly the same situation -- the period of transition between the conciliar system of government and that of the cabinet or ministerial council. But imitation may have played a role as well in this process: when Leopold wrote to Count Pötting in 1668 about meetings of a few Privy Councillors he made reference to "Juntas": You yourself know that the most important matters and particularly negotiations involving Spain or the House of Austria are never discussed *in pleno* but only in Conferences or Juntas in which only five or six Councillors are used."[26]

Now that we have some idea of the significance of the Deputation and of the extent to which it was a generally European phenomenon it may help to provide us with some enlightenment on the nature of the Austrian government in the time of Leopold I and the mentality that reigned in the rarefied circle of the Emperor and his chief ministers and advisers. The use of the term 'Habsburg absolutism' has already been noted in the expectation that the history of the Deputation might be of some assistance in clarifying its meaning and probable value as an *omnium gatherum* for Austrian government and society in this very period. 'Habsburg absolutism' has recently become a matter of some concern for specialists in this period who are not Austrians but Czechs and Hungarians. In these two countries something like an historiographical consensus has begun to emerge, and 'Habsburg absolutism' has come to mean a fusion of the dynasty and the great landowning class, a compromise of the Habsburgs and the wealthy magnates. One scholar gives her understanding of the meaning of the term in this way:

> At the turn of the 17th and 18th centuries Habsburg absolutism represented the interests of the feudal ruling class and the state power became the means of a small ruling clique closing, thus, the ways which could have led to a free peasant life and forced back Hungary's people striving for freedom into a system of constant serfdom and oppression.[27]

An extended commentary on this text would lead us too far afield. One should note the Marxist underpinnings of this definition that is also a judgment of a kind, and, at the same time, remember that it was written from the vantage point of one of the component parts of the Austrian Monarchy -- the Hungarian national experience. When the necessary adjustments have been made for these factors in the discussion, it is possible to continue it in the light of some additional evidence, the protocols of the meetings of the Deputation.

There can be no doubt of the balance between centralism and federalism in the political order of Leopoldinian Austria. From the standpoint of the central administration the relationship to the nobility had to take into account the fact that this order of society remained the most powerful single force in the political and social sphere still cannot be reduced to a 'state power' that was simply at the beck and call of a 'small ruling clique'. The government had to work with the nobility; it could not conceive of dispensing with its presence and its contribution to the making of official policy. But other factors were at work as well, and one of them, the increased responsibilities that resulted from Austria's new Great Power status, occasionally forced the government to invade spheres that had usually been the monopoly of the local nobilities. Leopold's government maneuvered, then, in a confined area, but it did to maneuver. At the one pole there was the bankruptcy that would be its fate if it did not collect sufficient funds; at the other pole there was the resistance or the outright insurrection that would result if it did its collecting too efficiently and without sufficient respect for local sensibilities. It was not much of a choice, this oscillation between bankruptcy and rebellion, but it provided the activities of the government with a degree of interest that it might otherwise not have possessed.

How similar the situation in Austria in 1697 was to the situation in Spain in 1624, when the Conde-Duque Olivares urged his royal master to establish a greater degree of conformity among the *"multa regna"* of the great Spanish Monarchy. He hoped to see the heavy burden that had been borne for so long a time by Castile shifted to some degree to Aragon, and the "Union of Arms" which he hoped to create resembled the *fundus* and its quotas, though in Olivares' scheme the number of paid troops replaced the number of gulden. John Elliott, who has studied the attempted reforms of Olivares, might easily have been discussing the situation in the Austrian Monarchy nearly a century later, when he writes:

> In this way, what seemed at first sight to be the greatest weakness of the Habsburg system of government -- its need to obtain the acquiescence of the tra- ditional governing class in the provinces, and its consequent commitment to the preservation of the existing social order -- often proved to be its greatest source of strength, since the attractiveness of revolution was much diminished. In fact, it may have been precisely because the Spanish Monarchy was *not* centralized, uniform and closely integrated in the way Olivares desired, that it managed to survive for so long. The very looseness and flexibility of the system gave it a resilience which a more rigid structure would almost certainly have lacked.[28]

Austria had no Olivares, but it did have tentatives in the way of a "Union of Arms" that would have reduced the 'looseness and flexibility' that had preserved it for so long. 'Habsburg absolutism' seen against this background takes on a rather different aspect. If it was simply a government at the service of a landed interest it did not always live up to its reputation: the efforts of Olivares ended in the revolt of the Catalans; the efforts of the Deputation played a part in the origin of the Rákóczi Rebellion of 1703.

The protocols of the Deputation testify to the true complexity of the situation in Vienna. They reveal an aristocrat arguing for the sweeping taxatation of the nobility and a professional bureaucrat, the Secretary, convinced that reform was impossible because the local Diets preserved the initiative in their votes of supply. The Instructions reveal a juxtaposition of mentalities and world views, the new and the old in a strange and bewildering assortment. Perhaps it is at this level that the Deputation acquires its final significance. For though its records have no immediate bearing on the intellectual history of Austria they do cast a powerful light on that set of attitudes and emotional characteristics that distinguished the Austrian from the Englishman, the Spaniard, the Prussian, and the Russian. This popular *Weltanschauung* has been called 'Baroque' and 'Viennese', and it has often been suggested that many of the characteristics of the present-day inhabitant of Vienna derive from that earlier source, that what we encounter along the *Ring* was once the property of the aristocratic circles of the old Monarchy. A satisfactory phenomenology of this Viennese conscious-ness seen in its historical development must await some future Husserl. At the moment, there is evidence that suggests that the members of the Deputation had some of the traits that are now common to the city as a whole. If they did not suffer from an excess of Viennese charm, they did have a basic attitude toward life that was alternately hopeful and despairing, terribly serious and then insouciant, capable of quick improvisation and long periods of complete disinterest and apathy.

These Austrian ministers had lived in a perpetual state of emergency. They had little doubt that there were moments when the survival of the Monarchy came into serious question. Since chaos and confusion were all about them, they clung desperately to order, to what was traditional and familiar. They delighted in the sheer variety of the peoples and traditions that were under Habsburg rule, and at the same time they could manage to be cynical about them. Their culture was largely aesthetic rather than intellectual. They realized their own weaknesses better than those who visited them and judged them with so little real understanding. But it was survival under difficult conditions that was their chief interest ("*überstehen ist alles*", Rilke was to say), and for the members of the Deputation, for the latter-day Viennese that was rendered in the more usual phrase "*wursteln*", to manage to get on in the same old humdrum way.

Perhaps it was these traits and the cultus of survival without any particular pretension to grandeur that best explains the Leopoldinian system, that puts the modish 'Habsburg absolutism' into its proper perspective. Any political or social system when examined in the light of one institution, one group of men, one restricted social class loses much of its sharpness of outline and ease in interpretation. 'Habsburg absolutism' under the microscope of the Deputation takes on a different look than that which it has for those who read the reports on the conditions of the peasants. The situation was not stable; the compromise between the center and the peripheries of the Monarchy was not eternal; the law of political necessity acted in innumerable and often contradictory ways. What preserved this curious unity of thought and society was its confirmed love of tradition and the fact that it had not yet experienced a defeat of such magnitude to require fundamental change in political structures and in categories of the mind. Until the fateful awakening that Austria experienced on the loss of Silesia its rulers and ministers, the men of the Deputation included, were content, indeed could think of no other alternative, to pour the new wine of innovation into some of the oldest wineskins imaginable.

Notes

1. "Dominus Harrach refert, a sua Maie state seye der ungarische cantzler zu ihme verwiessen. Theils magnaten wären dahier, der palatinus habe mit selbigen die repartition machen wollen, isti autem noluissent, sed -- sicuti essent 6 partes regni: 1° Croatien, 2do Sclavonien, 3° disseits der Donaw, 4to jenseits der Donaw, 5to Oberungarn, 6to wass über der Theyss -- man mögte rescribiren, ut singuli districtus mittant huc suos homines.", *Dep. Prot. 1699*, Oct. 16, 1699, fol. 53-54.

2. "Dominus Cardinalis dicit, ess werde lang hergehen, die zeit leide ess nicht; wären vorm jahr 3 mahl beysammen gewesen, et tantum clamassent."; "Itaque domino cancellario et palatino dicendum, ut veniant una cum magnatibus, qui etiam adessent... (et) faciant repartitionem.", *ibid.*, the same session, fol. 54-55.

3. "Deinde graviter conqueruntur, quod nobilitas subiiciatur tributis, *ac si esset gregaria* (italics my own).", *ibid.*, Nov. 16, 1699, fol. 63-64.

4. "Volunt neoacquisitos comitatus tamquam regni membra ad contribuendum immatriculari. Wollen Croatien und Sclavonien auch darbey haben... Additur etiam, die Cammer solle keine Güter verkhauffen und die Ungarische Cantzley keine donationales ausafertigen, sondern Ihr May. die güter widergeben, ad quos antea pertinuissent.", *ibid.*, same session, fol. 64.

5. "Croatien und Sclavonien wären sub rubrica Ungarorum et cetera.",
ibid., Nov. 19, 1699, fol. 65.

6. "Dominus Cardinalis dicit, 3 millionen 200.000 fl. wurden begehrt
Darob müesse man halten... Concludit: Ess wäre zu wilnschen, das Ihr May: willfahren könten. Man habe aber die armada vonnöthen, könten also nit darvon nachlassen... Palatinus itaque dahin zu verbescheiden, sie müessten derzeit geduld tragen, man werde sie in andereweeg consoliren. NB: Hoc omnibus dicitur, sed nihil servatur (this grim afterthought is surely the Secretary's work).", *ibid.*, Dec. 22, 1699, fol. 74.

7. A *Relatio Commissionis Posoniensis* was discussed by the Deputation on Dec. 30, 1700, *Dep. Prot. 1700*, fol. 138.

7a. *Ibid.*, Sept. 16, 1700, fol. 187.

8. *Ibid.*, May 20, 1700, fol. 173.

9. "Dominus Cardinalis: Semper necessarius miles in Hungaria. Mani pulus rebellium ferme totam turbasset.", *Dep. Prot. 1698*, Feb. 14, 1698, fol. 9.

10. "Hofkriegsratspraesident: In Ungarn alles zu aufatand geneigt, also das landt nicht zu entblossen.", *Dep. Prot. 1700*, Oct. 26, 1700, fol. 154. The previous spring the question had been raised of sending troops Hungary to Bohemia, and the Deputation had

decided against such a move, "in Hungarn die gefahr allezeit vorhanden.", *ibid.*, May 4, 1700, fol. 30.

11. "Periculum modo maius esset illo, quod fuisset anno 1683.", *ibid.*, Jan. 7, 1701, fol. 130-131.

12. It is difficult to agree with so important an authority as Oswald Redlich in his statement: "Es war begreiflich, doch von ernsten Folgen, dass... die Regierung in Wien diesem Unwesen eine Bedeutung nicht beimassen und die Gefahr unterschätzten.", *Das Werden einer Grossmacht: Österreich von 1700 bis 1740* (Wien, 1942), 162.

13. "Herr graff von Kaunitz: *Man solle ein landt, wie das andere tractiren* (italics my own)...", *Dep. Prot. 1701*, April 12, 1701, fol. 13; again, "Kaunitz: Die länder, as möge in Ungarn oder in anderen sam, wan sie renitent, solle man sie mit der execution belegen.", *Dep. Prot. 1699*, Sept. 13, 1699, fol. 27-28.   Another Bohemian magnate who occasionally appeared in the Deputation, Count Czernin, indicated at one point the background for the Bohemian view: "Ess müess eine gleichheit zwischen denen ländern sein, sonsten würde denen Höhmischen hart geschehen.", *ibid.*, May 18, 1699, fol. 48.

14. "Die länder wären nicht gleich. Gott habe Steyrnarck nicht eben gemacht. Man müesse das brod nehmben, wie as seye."; this view was
expressed in a meeting of the Privy Conference, Sept. 19, 1697, *Voträge*, (Fasz. 36, 1697), fol. 83.

15. "Moverem ego (the Secretary), wegen schwtirigkeit dess adels: so er (Kardinal) widerlegt; man solle den adel nit förchten, mehrers 2,000 Bauern alsa einen Edelmann.", *Dep. Prot. 1698*, Nov. 4, 1698, tol. 237.

16. "Dominus Gundagger: Wan die bewilligung stabiliert, wolle er geld aufbringen.", *Dep. Prot. 1699*, May 18, 1699, fol. 28.

17. The point made by Count San Martino, the Piedmontese minister in Vienna (1717), *Relazioni di Ambasciatori Sabaudi, Genovesi e Veneti (1693-1713)*, ed. Carlo Morondi (Bologna, 1935), I, 128.

18. "Ötting dicit, dominus Gundacker koste 200.000 fl. (cipher), *Dep. Prot. 1699*, Oct. 12, 1699, fol. 52. The Palatine complained at the very end of 1699 that his salary as a general was in arrears -- 30,000 gulden. He found this all the more annoying because Gundacker Starhemberg "hätte so viehl und er so wenig.", *ibid.*, Dec. 30, 1699, 76.

19. Kollonich exprressed his keen annoyance with Count Jörger, the head of the Lower Austrian Regiment, because he had spoken up for special treatment of the Austrians. The Primate of Hungary believed that all the lands should be treated as equals and that the Austrians should not be favored by the government, *Dep. Prot. 1700*, Jan. 7, 1701, fol. 131.

20. "Die Landtsverfassungen seint nit gleich, lassen sich nit übern hauffen werffen.",

Dep. Prot. 1699, May 18, 1699, fol. 27.

21. Session of the Privy Conference, Nov. 12, 1699, *Vorträge*, (Fasz. 37, 1699-1700), fol.   207-208.

22. H. Haussherr, *Verwaltungseinheit und Ressorttrennung vom Ende des 17. bis zum Beginn des 19. Jahrhunderts* (Berlin, 1953), 69.

23. For the *Juntas*, cf. J. Elliott, Imperial Spain: 1469-1716 (London, 1964), 317ff.

24. H. Antoine, "Les comités de Kinistres sous le règne de Louis XV," *Revue historique du Droit francais et etranger*, LVII (1951), 193-230.

25. R. A. Dorwart, *The Administrative Reforms of Frederick William I of Prussia* (Cambridge, Mass., 1953), esp.162-164.

26. H. F. Schwarz, *The Imperial Privy Council in the Seventeenth Century* (Cambridge, Mass., 1943), 172.

27. The most important articles having to do with the current interest in the nature of 'Habsburg absolutism' are the following: F. Kavka, "Die Habsburger und der böhmische Staat bis zur Mitte des 18. Jahrhunderts," *Historica*, VIII (1964), 57-72, and the articles published in the collection *Études Historiques* (Budapest, 1960), esp. L. Makkai, "Die Entstehung der gesellschaftlichen Basis des Absolutismus in den Ländern der österreichischen Habsburger", I, 627-668, and in the more recent *Nouvelles études historiques* (Budapest, 1965) I. Wellmann, "Merkanti. ische Vorstellungen im 17. Jahrhundert und Ungarn, 315-354, Á. Várkonyi, "Habsburg Absolutism and Serfdom in Hungary at the Turn of the XVIIth and XVIIIth Centuries, 355-388, Gy. Ember, "Zur Klassenpolitik des Habsburger-absolutismus in Ungarn in den sechziger Jahren des 18. Jahrhunderts", 389-414. The definition of 'Habsburg absolutism' is taken from the Várkonyi article, 387.

28. J. H. Elliott, *The Revolt of the Catalans: A Study in the Decline of Spain: 1598-1640* (Cambridge, 1963), 546-547.